D0585600

Fondues

Fondues

Sonia Allison

PIATKUS

© 1989 Sonia Allison

First published in 1989 by
Judy Piatkus (Publishers) Limited
5 Windmill St, London W1P 1HF

British Library Cataloguing in Publication Data
Allison, Sonia
  Fondues.
  1. Food : Fondue dishes – Recipes
  I. Title
  641, 8

  ISBN 0-86188-891-X

Designed by Paul Saunders
Illustrations by Anne Ormerod

Photoset in $11\frac{1}{2}$/13pt Lasercomp Palatino
Printed and bound at the Alden Press
Oxford London and Northampton

To my cousins Vivian and George, gourmets par excellence, who will surely eat their way through this book with the utmost pleasure.

And to Helen, another cousin in Switzerland, for introducing me to fondues all those years ago.

Contents

LIST OF COLOUR ILLUSTRATIONS

opposite page

Introduction

*F*ondues are party pieces par excellence. In Switzerland – where they are the national dish – they are served après ski to holiday-makers and winter revellers alike. At home they are an ideal means of entertaining informally, bringing people together in an atmosphere of jovial bonhomie.

What is a fondue? It is a rich and creamy melt of cheese with a million and one additions. Blissful.

The origins of cheese fondue would appear to go back far in history. One version is said to date back to the Ancient Romans and was based on what amounted to a warm concoction made from goats' cheese and a raw, almost crudish wine. Hundreds of

years later, Brillat-Savarin, the great eighteenth-century chef, pronounced the fondue a Swiss thoroughbred – although he seemed to confuse it with a scrambled-egg mixture flavoured with cheese! In nineteenth-century Britain, fondues were taken to be feather-light French savouries baked in individual paper cases and made from Gruyère and Parmesan cheeses enriched with egg yolks and fluffed with stiffly beaten whites. There were variations with Stilton cheese and an abundance of Parmesan but the closest one to the Swiss, as we understand it, was a Gruyère cheese fondue endowed with slices of luxurious white truffles (sniffed out by pigs in English woods and forests) and referred to in *Cassell's Dictionary of Food* (circa 1899) as expensive – and at 'six shillings to eighteen shillings a pound' truffles were indeed. Famous nineteenth-century cooks, including Mrs Rundell, Francatelli and even witty and genial Soyer who was almost prophetic in his understanding and knowledge of food, thought fondues and soufflés one and the same. And even in the early part of this century, a cookery writer called Nancy Lake desribed *fondue au Parmesan* as 'a cheese fondue, baked in a soufflé dish or paper case, or steamed.' The book was a gem, called *Menus Made Easy*, and was published in 1901 by Frederick Warne.

When a fondue actually became a fondue, melted rather than baked, is unclear. What we do know for certain is that fondue was, and is, a Swiss-French term for an economical meal made during winter by farming communities all over central Europe as a means of using up last year's cheese.

Early on, the cheese was melted down with home-brewed wine in a cauldron-shaped pan; later the Swiss adopted a shallowish pan, or *caquelon*, which was placed over a spirit stove to keep hot. The melt was scooped up with crusty pieces of freshly baked bread speared onto long, fork-like implements. Although it was considered unpretentious and uncomplicated, this cheese fondue provided nourishment, sustenance and warmth to hardworking country folk. Today fondue is known in the Netherlands as kaasdoop (cheese dip) and in Italy as fonduta.

The traditional Swiss fondue is made using Emmental, Gruyère and Appenzal cheeses with white wine and kirsch. However if purists are alarmed at the variety of cheeses and alcohols I suggest in this book, take heart. I asked one of the chefs at the Swiss Centre in London if I could vary the types of cheeses, wines and spirits in the fondues. He thought for a minute. 'Vy not?,' he said, in his best Swiss-German English, shrugging his shoulders at my apparent ignorance. However, for greater authenticity, use cheeses and wines from the same country wherever possible. Italian cheese, Italian wine; German cheese, German wine; English cheese, English wine.

Quaint Swiss customs exist concerning fondues. It is a long standing tradition that if a man drops his bread into the fondue he must buy a bottle of wine for all the guests. If a lady does the same, she must kiss all the men present on the cheek. If anyone drops their bread for a second time, then they must host the next fondue party.

There are other kinds of fondues apart from cheese. The popular and sophisticated Fondue Bourguignonne is made by frying cubes of tender steak at the table in a pan of oil over a spirit stove. According to one of my contemporaries who is well-versed in the higher realms of haute cuisine, the whole thing is an import from Burgundy. Perhaps. In an unburgundian fashion, the fried meat is eaten with chips, pickles and a selection of cold sauces made from a base of mayonnaise, cream, yogurt or puréed vegetables. These act as dips.

Fondue Chinoise, or Chinese Fondue, is another variation but this time thin slices of beef, veal or turkey breast are simmered in stock at the table, not fried. Any liquid which remains at the end, beautifully flavoured from the meat by now, is divided between the participants and drunk as soup.

There are sweet fondues too, made from soft cheeses, fudge, marshmallows and even fruit purées. The most fashionable and chic is a pan of chocolate fondue. It is a glorification of a dream dessert made from white, milk or dark chocolate and often laced with liqueurs and an assortment of additions ranging from finely chopped walnuts or toasted coconut to the finest of fine grated orange zest or preserved ginger. Originally it was thought of as something to delight children at birthday parties but the thought of chocolatey fingers up and down best clothes is too torturous to contemplate. Keep it for grown-ups.

Here are fondues to suit every taste and every occasion. *Bon appetit* and *bon chance*!

Cheese File

You will find all the cheeses featured in the recipes explained in the following glossary. Availability can vary, so be prepared to shop around when looking for a particular cheese. Supermarkets, specialist cheese shops and market stalls all carry an impressive range of British and international cheeses.

Some cheeses, particularly the soft creamy textured ones, can be more easily grated if they are kept in the refrigerator until the last minute. You may even find it easier to slice and chop certain cheeses rather than grate.

APPENZELLER

A Swiss, cow's milk cheese made originally in the canton of Appenzell as long ago as the twelfth century but now also produced in Thurgau and St Gall. The cheese is semi-hard, peppered with smallish holes, creamy textured and full flavoured.

APPLEWOOD

A type of Cheddar cheese that has been smoked over applewood, hence the name. It has a delicate smoked flavour and a brown rind which is edible.

BEL PAESE

An Italian cow's milk cheese made in northern Italy and renowned for its delicacy and soft texture. It is a 'young' cheese that takes only 6–8 weeks to mature. The name means beautiful country. Refrigeration is essential.

BLUE CHESHIRE

A British cow's milk cheese which is soft and crumbly. The veins are actually green rather than blue. Its flavour is rich and tangy.

BRIE

One of France's most famous cheeses, Brie can be traced back to the eighth century and is now being copied all over Europe. Fairly flat and white skinned, it is made from cow's milk and has a soft, creamy texture and mild but piquant flavour. Avoid overripe Brie, especially if it smells of ammonia.

CAERPHILLY

A British cow's milk cheese originally made in Wales in the eighteenth century but now almost exclusively produced in England. It is available as a pasteurised and unpasteurised cheese. Caerphilly matures in 2 weeks and is white, mild, moist, a tiny bit acidic and easy to digest. It may be used instead of Feta cheese, which it slightly resembles in taste and texture. The cheese crumbles easily and grating is not always necessary.

CAMEMBERT

A distinctively-flavoured Normandy cheese which was first produced at the beginning of the eighteenth century. The best Camembert is made from unpasteurised cow's milk and bears a label carrying the terms 'fermier' and/or 'lait cru'. Sold in whole rounds or in halves, it should be plump and resilient to the touch with a white or creamy white rind flecked with red. It has a positive flavour and aroma. Avoid Camembert that has sunk in the middle and smells of ammonia as this indicates that it is past its prime.

CHEDDAR

A firm cow's milk cheese which is full-fat (48%), full-flavoured, generally mellow, golden yellow and with a smooth texture. Its strength lies in the length of time it has been left to mature, which can be anything from 3 months to one year. Although Cheddar started out as English, it is now produced worldwide.

CHESHIRE (RED, WHITE)

Said to be Britain's oldest cheese, the production of Cheshire goes back to pre-Roman times when the North of England was inhabited by Celtic tribes. It is mellow, slightly tangy and fresh tasting, and is ideal for cooking. The cheese crumbles readily and there are Red (actually orange), and White varieties. It has the same fat content as Cheddar. See also BLUE CHESHIRE.

DANBO

A mild, creamy coloured Danish cheese made from cow's milk. It has a firm texture and is dotted with holes. It is left to ripen for 5 months.

DANISH BLUE (DANABLU)

A sharpish and fairly salty cow's milk cheese threaded with blue veins. Almost white and fairly crumbly, Danish Blue is considered strong.

DERBY

An English cow's milk cheese with a close, flaky texture. It is pale coloured and has a mild flavour. SAGE DERBY contains the juice of sage leaves.

DOUBLE GLOUCESTER

A fine, mellow and buttery tasting cheese with a flaky texture. It is still produced in creameries, but these days is dyed bright orange with a natural dye called annatto. Once upon a time it was made only from cow's milk of Gloucester black cattle and the word 'double' refers to its size, hence the name, and because Double Gloucester used to be twice the size of single Gloucester.

EDAM

A cow's milk cheese, produced in the Netherlands in the fourteenth century and named after the town where it was first made. It is traditionally ball shaped with a vivid red overcoat. The texture is firm and supple, the colour deepish gold and the flavour medium strong.

EMMENTAL

One of Switzerland's top cheeses, used both for cooking and dessert. Mild and nutty tasting, this cow's milk cheese is characterised by fairly large holes throughout its texture and is firm and easy to slice. The rind is brownish-yellow and the production of Emmental is emulated worldwide.

ESROM

A cow's milk cheese from Denmark with a fairly firm texture and dotted with irregularly shaped holes. It is mild yet piquant at the same time and is used in cold meals, sandwiches and cooking.

FETA (FETTA)

A centuries-old cheese produced mainly in the Balkans, primarily Greece. Originally made from ewe's milk, it is now also produced from goat's and cow's milk. It has a fairly firm, crumbly texture and the taste is on the sharp side, slightly acidic and a bit salty. It is a well-loved cooking cheese in its country of origin, where it is also used to decorate salads.

GJETOST

Unique from Norway, this is a caramel-coloured cheese made from whey – 10% goats and 90% cow's. It is mild, sweetish, very smoothly-textured and perfect in sandwiches – children love it. It is also an excellent cooking cheese and makes a superb fondue.

GORGONZOLA

A fairly strong Italian blue cheese that is akin to British Stilton and French Roquefort. It has a smooth and creamy texture and is produced in Lombardy from cow's milk. It is creamy yellow in colour.

GOUDA

A famous cow's milk Dutch cheese, dating back to the thirteenth century. When sold young, between 1 and 4 months old, it tastes mild and creamy but as it matures the flavour intensifies and becomes strong and piquant. It is a medium-firm, golden coloured cheese which is supple and easy to slice. The odd hole is here and there. It is named after the town of original production.

GRUYÈRE

A top-quality cow's milk cheese from Switzerland first produced in the twelfth century. Gruyère is a fine-quality classic cheese and respected internationally. It has a mild flavour and creamy texture with a few small holes and is easy to slice. Gruyère is a popular fondue cheese and is also eaten for dessert.

HALLOUMI

A fairly hard, salty cheese from the Middle East. It is made from ewe's or goat's milk, is almost white in colour and preserved in whey. It is used primarily for cooking.

HAVARTI

A rindless Danish cheese, full-flavoured and pungent, named after the farm where it was originally produced. It is made from cow's milk, medium-firm, and dotted with small holes. It can be round like Dutch Gouda or shaped into oblong loaves. Sometimes the cheese contains caraway seeds.

JARLSBERG

Norway's equivalent of Emmental, though it tastes more like a cross between Gouda and Edam.

LANCASHIRE

A well-loved English cheese with a soft, crumbly texture and a deliciously fresh tang. Lancashire is made from cow's milk and may be used as a cooking or dessert cheese. It goes beautifully with fresh pears and apples.

LYMESWOLD

New-on-the-scene cow's milk English cheeses in three varieties: Mild Blue Lymeswold, Lymeswold English County Brie and Creamy White Lymeswold. They are quality cheeses used for cooking and dessert.

MANCHEGO

A high-quality Spanish ewe's milk cheese which has a firm texture and a mild, creamy taste. It is one of Spain's most popular cheeses.

MOZZARELLA

Italy's 'pizza' cheese, originally made 400 years ago from buffalo's milk but now produced from cow's milk. It is pliable, packed in smallish pieces and off-white in colour. It is naturally elastic and becomes stretchy when freshly cooked. Mozzarella is copied worldwide but the best variety comes directly from Italy, sealed in bags of whey.

MYCELLA

A mild, blue-veined Danish cow's milk cheese with a rich and creamy taste and texture. It is milder and smoother than Danish Blue.

PARMESAN

A hard, granite-like and close-textured cow's milk cheese made in northern Italy. When very fresh it may be treated as a dessert cheese and eaten with fresh fruit and nuts. As it matures and hardens, grating is recommended. It is very full-flavoured and a little goes a long way. Once grated, it should be kept in an airtight container in the refrigerator.

PECORINO

A superb-tasting Italian sheep's milk cheese, recommended for cooking and dessert. It is firm textured, thickly rinded and popular in Italy.

PORT SALUT

A French cow's milk cheese, first made 200 years ago by Trappist monks of the Port-du-Salut Abbey at Entrammes. It has a mild flavour and a soft, smooth texture and is useful both as a dessert and cooking cheese. It is now factory produced.

PROVOLONE

A hardish cow's milk cheese from Italy with a piquant flavour. It is left to mature for anything from 6 months to 2 years and the maturer cheeses are widely used in cooking.

PYRÉNÉES

A mild and creamy tasting French cheese made from cow's or sheep's milk in the mountainous South West. The cheese made from cow's milk is black skinned, while that made from sheep's milk has an orange rind. The texture is supple, dotted with small holes and the colour is pale cream.

RACLETTE

Raclette is the name of a Swiss cow's milk cheese widely used in cooking. It is mild in taste, similar to Gruyère, melts easily and is also the name of a classic Swiss dish — Raclette. This is made by melting the cut side of half a wheel of the cheese in front of a small electric fire. Melting slices are scraped on to a plate and eaten with boiled potatoes and pickles. The cheese is now produced in France.

RED LEICESTER

A medium-hard English cow's milk cheese, dyed reddish-orange with natural annatto. It has a mild, fresh flavour and can be used in cooking or as a dessert cheese.

RICOTTA

An Italian whey cheese that is snow white, mild in taste, high in protein, low in fat and easy to digest. To increase its nutritional value, whole or semi-skimmed milk is sometimes added during production. British versions are usually unsalted and bland.

RIDDER

A Norwegian cow's milk cheese that resembles Port Salut in flavour and texture.

SAMSØ

This is Denmark's national cheese. It is made from cow's milk and its flavour resembles English Cheddar and Emmental combined. It is excellent for cooking and as a dessert cheese.

SMOKED CHEESE

Usually from Germany, this is a processed or unprocessed cheese that has been naturally smoked. It is splendid for eating and cooking and makes a superb fondue.

STILTON

An English blue cheese that is rated as the King of all cheeses. It was originally produced in Leicestershire 200 years ago from cow's milk. It is carefully protected by the Stilton Cheese Making Association and only Stiltons produced in the shire counties of Leicester, Nottingham and Derby are considered genuine. The cheese itself is mild and slightly crumbly, pale cream in colour and mottled with blue-green veins. As the cheese ripens and strengthens in taste, the colour turns to dark cream and the texture becomes less crumbly and more paste-like. WHITE STILTON is young Stilton (6–8 weeks old) that has not had culture added to it. Thus it stays white with a fresh and tingly flavour.

SVENBO

A Danish version of Emmental.

TOMME DE SAVOIE

A mild and supple cow's milk cheese produced in the Haute-Savoie region of France. It can be made from whole or semi-skimmed milk.

WENSLEYDALE

Made from cow's milk this is an English cheese which ripens in 3–4 weeks. It is tangy, white and crumbly and eaten in the North country with apple pie. It is excellent in cooking.

The Bread Basket

*A*lthough the range of shop-bought breads is vast and still growing, novelty breads need a personal touch and my selection is different from the run-of-the-mill supermarket choice and well suited to fondues. All are made from the same basic recipe using easy-mix yeast which gives no trouble and produces super bread.

Where one of the breads goes well with a particular fondue, this has been indicated in the recipe.

BASIC CRUSTY BREAD

This is my basic recipe to which extra ingredients can be added to vary the taste (see opposite and page 26)

MAKES 2 LOAVES

$1\frac{1}{2}$ lb (750 g) strong plain white, brown, stoneground or granary flour
2 level teaspoons salt
1 oz (25 g) butter, margarine, or vegetable cooking fat
1 sachet easy-blend yeast
$\frac{1}{4}$ pint (150 ml) boiling water and $\frac{1}{2}$ pint (275 ml) cold water, mixed

1. Sift the flour and salt into a bowl. Tip any bran left in the sieve into the bowl. Rub in the butter, margarine or fat until the mixture resembles fine breadcrumbs. Sprinkle in the yeast.

2. Add the warm water and mix to softish dough. Turn out on to a well-floured surface.

3. Knead for about 10 minutes until the dough is smooth and elastic and no longer sticky. Shape into a ball.

4. Return the dough to an oiled bowl, cover with oiled cling film or foil and leave in a warm place for 45 minutes to 1 hour, or until doubled in size.

5. Turn out on to a floured surface and knead lightly for 2 to 3 minutes. Cut the dough in half.

6. Knead your chosen flavourings into each piece of dough, flouring the work surface and your hands as often as is needed.

7. Shape each piece into a ball, place on a greased and floured baking sheet and leave in a warm place until doubled in size. This can take anything from 15 to 45 minutes, depending on the temperature.

8. Heat the oven to 230° C/450° F/Gas Mark 8 and bake the loaves for 25 to 30 minutes or until well browned and hollow sounding when tapped on the base.

9. Leave to cool on a wire rack before eating.

Sesame and Fennel Seed Bread
Add $\frac{1}{2}$ oz (15 g) sesame seeds and 1 level teaspoon fennel seeds to half the dough.

Orange and Date Bread
Add 1 level teaspoon finely grated orange peel and 2 oz (50 g) chopped dates to half the dough.

Lemon and Raisin Bread
Add 1 level teaspoon finely grated lemon peel and $1\frac{1}{2}$ oz (40 g) raisins to half the dough.

Lemon and Walnut Bread
Add 1 level teaspoon finely grated lemon peel and $1\frac{1}{2}$ oz (40 g) finely chopped walnuts to half the dough.

Hazelnut and Nutmeg Bread
Add $1\frac{1}{2}$ oz (40 g) toasted and finely chopped hazelnuts and $\frac{1}{4}$ level teaspoon nutmeg to half the dough.

Anchovy and Chive Bread
Add 1 teaspoon anchovy purée, essence or sauce and 2 level tablespoons dried chives to half the dough.

Chilli Bread
Add 2 level teaspoons mild chilli seasoning to half the dough.

Mustard Bread
Add 2 level teaspoons mustard powder to half the dough.

Oriental Bread
Add 1 level teaspoon cumin seeds and 2 level teaspoons medium-hot curry powder to half the dough.

Spicy Bread
Add 1 level teaspoon cumin seeds and 2 level teaspoons dill seeds to half the dough.

Italian Bread
Add $1\frac{1}{2}$ tablespoons tomato purée and 1 level teaspoon garlic granules to half the dough.

Mixed Seed Bread
Add 1 tablespoon mustard seeds, fried in $\frac{1}{2}$ tablespoon hot oil for about 45 seconds or until they go 'pop, pop, pop', and 2 tablespoons poppy seeds to half the dough.

Onion Bread
Add 2 oz (50 g) finely chopped and lightly fried onions to half the dough.

Pickle Bread
Add 2 tablespoons pickle, such as Ploughman's, to half the dough.

Hungarian Bread
Add 2 oz (50 g) chopped and lightly toasted almonds and 2 level teaspoons paprika to half the dough.

Savoury
Cheese Fondues

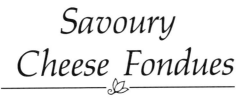

*T*he most traditional fondues are those made from cheese. The cheese is melted in a shallow pan or *caquelon* which is then transferred to a spirit stove in the centre of the dining table from which the diners help themselves.

The fondue is a fairly thin consistency when it is taken to the table and it gradually thickens up during the meal. The crust that forms across the bottom of the pan is considered a great delicacy by the Swiss, who scrape it up with their bread. Should you, by chance, have any fondue left over you can always turn it into cheese on toast for a meal the next day.

It is a tradition in Switzerland that everyone gulps back a glass

of icy kirsch, known as the *coupe de milieu*, halfway through eating the fondue. It is best to avoid other icy cold drinks with a cheese fondue and I find the most acceptable aid to digestion is hot, soothing lemon tea. If you do want to serve white wine, it should be cool rather than chilled and preferably the same type used in the fondue.

Not all cheese fondues contain alcohol and the recipes beginning on page 74 use alternative liquids such as milk, yogurt or non-alcoholic wine. These fondues are more suitable for the 'don't drink and drive' brigade.

Read the cookery notes on the following pages before making a fondue for the first time.

COOKERY HINTS

Equipment
For a cheese fondue, use a traditional *caquelon* (fondue pot) if you have one. This is usually made from enamelled cast iron, copper aluminium and sometimes stainless steel. You can always improvise if you don't have one, as long as you remember that the pot should be flameproof with a short handle on one side and a fairly thick base to prevent the fondue burning on the bottom. It should sit comfortably on a well-balanced spirit stove. Do not use anything that could be a possible fire hazard — such as a pan with a long handle that could easily be knocked over.

Stand the spirit stove on mats as the base may get very hot. Instead of a spirit stove you can use an electric plate warmer which should be set to a medium heat. An electric wok could also be used for melting and heating the fondue but keep the heat setting fairly low. Whatever you use, it should be placed at one end of the table or where it is within everyone's easy reach. Remember to provide your guests with long-handled fondue forks (which look like skewers with pronged ends).

The microwave cooker, now a fact of life in the modern kitchen, can successfully be used to melt the fondue and I give general instructions opposite.

Le Saucier is a thermostatically controlled electric pan with no handles. It has a built-in paddle which stirs the contents as they are heating and is perfect for small fondues. Instructions for its use are on page 73.

Watch-points

Follow the instructions in each recipe carefully. In particular, be sure to stir the fondue continuously once you have added the cheese. It is also important that you do not allow the mixture to over-boil or it may turn stringy. To avoid this, transfer the pot to your spirit stove as soon as the mixture has come to the boil and thickened to a smooth and creamy consistency.

Do not be tempted to add alcohol to a fondue containing ewe's or goat's milk cheese; they do not mix but separate out into a runny liquid and a lumpy mass. Some cheeses are very salty, so add salt sparingly and only where given in a recipe.

Rescue Remedies

If a cheese fondue appears to be separating out, work in a generous squeeze of lemon juice.

If a cheese fondue doesn't thicken, stir in 1–2 level teaspoons of cornflour mixed to a smooth paste with a little extra liquid. This can be wine, milk or even water.

To Cook in the Microwave

A cheese fondue can successfully be melted in a microwave cooker and transferred to a spirit stove at the table. Do ensure that the dish in which you cook the fondue is suitable for use in a microwave cooker as well as being flameproof.

The instructions given are for a 600 watt oven.

1. Place all the ingredients except the spirit into a flameproof microwave dish.

2. Leave the dish uncovered and cook at full power for about 6–8 minutes or until the fondue starts to bubble gently, stirring every $1\frac{1}{2}$ minutes.

3. Remove from the oven and blend in the spirit, if applicable. Transfer the dish to a spirit stove and eat straight away with your chosen 'dippers'.

VEGETABLES FOR DIPPING

The traditional 'dippers' to eat with savoury cheese fondues are cubes of crusty bread. There are, additionally, a wide choice of other ingredients that can serve admirably as 'dippers' and in each recipe I have given my own suggestions for the most appropriate ones for the specific fondue. Of course it is all a matter of personal taste.

The following vegetables all make excellent 'dippers' and, again, they are simply suggestions to give you ideas. For my own taste, I cook some vegetables until tender and only par-boil others (such as cauliflower) so that there is still a bit of crunch and texture left to contrast with the softness of the melted cheese.

Canned artichoke hearts, well drained. Serve warm or cold.

Broccoli, par-boiled. Serve warm or cold.

Brussels sprouts, cooked until just tender. Serve warm.

Carrots, thickly sliced and par-boiled or cooked until just tender. Serve warm.

Cauliflower, par-boiled. Serve warm.

Celeriac, cut into cubes and boiled in salted water to which 3 teaspoons of lemon juice have been added to prevent discoloration. Serve warm.

Celery, cut diagonally into short lengths. Serve raw.

Courgettes, cut into medium-thick slices. Par-boil until just tender but not floppy. Serve warm.

Fennel, cut into pieces and par-boiled in salted water to which 3 teaspoons of lemon juice have been added to prevent discoloration. Serve warm.

Kohlrabi, cut into cubes and boiled in salted water to which 3 teaspoons of lemon juice have been added to prevent discoloration. Serve warm.

Button mushrooms, trimmed. Serve raw.

Peppers, cut into squares. Par-boil in salted water. Serve warm.

Roots, these include parsnips, turnips, swedes and potatoes. Cut into cubes and cook in boiling salted water until tender. Serve warm.

Squash, this includes marrow and pumpkin. Cube and par-boil in salted water. Serve warm.

Baby sweetcorn, snap in half and cook in boiling salted water for 3–4 minutes. Serve warm.

SAVOURY CHEESE FONDUES WITH ALCOHOL

SWISS CHEESE FONDUE

*T*his is the one that fondue addicts know best and perhaps love most. The true and traditional brew should contain Royal and Vacherin cheeses in addition to the Emmental, Gruyère and App-enzeller used here. But, as they are so hard to find (my favourite and well-patronised cheese stalls at Watford and Oxford markets don't stock them on a regular basis, so I know availability is a problem), I simply increase the quantities of the other three more readily available cheeses and still make a fine fondue with a Swiss air of respectability. If any of you know of a specialist cheese shop from where Royal and Vacherin cheeses are obtainable, please write and tell me!

SERVES 4

1 garlic clove, peeled and halved
8 fl. oz (225 ml) Swiss white wine
8 oz (225 g) Emmental cheese, de-rinded and finely grated
6 oz (175 g) Gruyère cheese, de-rinded and finely grated
2 oz (50 g) Appenzeller cheese, de-rinded and finely grated
1 teaspoon lemon juice
1 level tablespoon cornflour
1 fl. oz (25 ml) kirsch

FOR DIPPING
cubes of wholemeal bread

1. Rub the cut sides of garlic over the base and sides of the fondue pot.

2. Add the wine and heat until hot. Mix in the grated cheeses and lemon juice.

3. Cook over a medium heat, stirring all the time, until the cheese melts and the mixture just begins to bubble.

4. Blend the cornflour to a thin paste with kirsch. Add to the cheese mixture and cook slowly, still stirring, until the mixture comes to the boil and thickens to a smooth and creamy consistency. Do not over-boil or the mixture may become stringy.

5. Stand the fondue pot over a spirit stove and eat straight away with cubes of wholemeal bread for a typical Swiss meal.

Fondue Valaisanne

Swiss Cheese Fondue served with bread cubes and air-cured beef, which, for an authentic Fondue Valaisanne, should come from the Engadine region. However, Parma ham is easier to find and can be substituted successfully.

Fondue Paysanne

Swiss Cheese Fondue served with Swiss sausages and new potatoes. A selection of other sausages may be substituted; pieces of Frankfurters, squares of Salami, top-quality pork sausages fried and cut into wedges, and cubes of the very best ham you can find.

Fondue aux Pommes

Swiss Cheese Fondue served with cubes of peeled apples instead of bread.

Fondue au Curry

Swiss Cheese Fondue to which 2–3 level teaspoons Madras curry powder are added immediately after the cornflour mixture.

Fondue Moitie-Moitié

Swiss Cheese Fondue served with new potatoes, cubed bread and raw button mushrooms.

Fondue Dijonaise

Swiss Cheese Fondue to which 2–3 teaspoons Dijon mustard are added immediately after the cornflour mixture.

Fondue aux Fines Herbes

Swiss Cheese Fondue to which 1 tablespoon herbes de Provence are added immediately after the cornflour mixture.

Fondue aux Verdures

Swiss Cheese Fondue served with pieces of seasonal, par-boiled green vegetables.

LUXURY SMOKED SALMON FONDUE

This is top of the range and perfect for entertaining. Eat with pieces of brioche or other rich white breads containing egg.

SERVES 4–6

8 fl. oz (225 ml) white wine
8 oz (225 g) Gruyère cheese, de-rinded and finely grated
8 oz (225 g) Emmental cheese, de-rinded and finely grated
1 level tablespoon cornflour
2 fl. oz (50 ml) gin
3 oz (75 g) smoked salmon, finely chopped

FOR DIPPING
pieces of brioche

1. Pour the wine into the fondue pot and heat until hot. Mix in the grated cheeses.

2. Cook over a medium heat, stirring all the time, until the cheeses melt and the mixture just begins to bubble.

3. Blend the cornflour to a thin paste with the gin and add to the cheese mixture.

4. Cook slowly, still stirring, until the mixture comes to the boil and thickens to a smooth and creamy consistency. Do not over-boil or it may become stringy. Stir in the smoked salmon.

5. Stand the fondue pot over a spirit stove and eat straight away with pieces of brioche.

Luxury Prawn Fondue

Make as above, substituting 3 oz (75 g) finely chopped prawns for the smoked salmon.

PYRÉNÉES FONDUE

This is a superb production with its own brand of sophistication, for adults only. Poire William spirit uplifts the soul and flavour, making the fondue a perfect foil for a very fresh baguette cut into cubes.

SERVES 4

1 garlic clove, peeled and halved
8 fl. oz (225 ml) white wine
1 teaspoon lemon juice
10 oz (275 g) Pyrénées cheese, de-rinded and finely grated
6 oz (175 g) Emmental cheese, de-rinded and finely grated
1 level tablespoon cornflour
2 tablespoons Poire William spirit (a colourless spirit similar to schnapps)

FOR DIPPING
cubes of crusty French bread or homemade Oriental Bread (page 25)

1. Rub the cut sides of garlic over the base and sides of the fondue pot. Pour in the wine and lemon juice and heat until hot. Mix in the grated cheeses.

2. Cook over a medium heat, stirring all the time, until the cheeses melt and the mixture just begins to bubble.

3. Blend the cornflour to a thin paste with the Poire William spirit and add to the cheese mixture.

4. Cook slowly, still stirring, until the mixture comes to the boil and thickens to a smooth and creamy consistency. Do not over-boil or it may become stringy.

5. Stand the fondue pot over a spirit stove and eat straight away with cubes of crusty French bread.

Pyrénées Fondue à la Framboise
Make as above but instead of Poire William, use the same amount of framboise (raspberry) spirit for a subtle hint of raspberry.

FRENCH FONDUE IN SWISS MOOD

A dream of French fragrance and a comfortably potent Fondue based on French-made, Swiss-style cheeses. Also included is Calvados (apple brandy and readily available in supermarkets), apple juice and a hint of garlic.

SERVES 4

1 garlic clove, peeled and halved
5 fl. oz (150 ml) Calvados
5 fl. oz (150 ml) apple juice
6 oz (175 g) French Raclette cheese, de-rinded and finely grated
10 oz (275 g) French Emmental cheese, de-rinded and finely grated
1 teaspoon lemon juice
1 level tablespoon cornflour

FOR DIPPING
cubes of crusty French bread or homemade Lemon and Walnut Bread
(page 25)

1. Rub the cut sides of garlic over the base and sides of the fondue pot. Pour in the Calvados and 4 fl. oz (120 ml) of the apple juice and heat until hot. Mix in the grated cheeses and lemon juice.

2. Cook over medium heat, stirring all the time, until the cheeses melt and the mixture just begins to bubble.

3. Blend the cornflour to a thin paste with the remaining apple juice and add to the cheese mixture.

4. Cook slowly, still stirring, until the mixture comes to the boil and thickens to a smooth and creamy consistency. Do not over-boil or it may become stringy.

5. Stand the fondue pot over a spirit stove and eat straight away with cubes of very fresh French bread.

Touch-of-Style French Fondue

Make as French Fondue in Swiss Mood, adding 2 tablespoons of chopped Madagascan green peppercorns (which are usually packed in jars) with the cornflour and apple juice.

Mustardy French Fondue

Make as French Fondue in Swiss Mood, adding 1 tablespoon ready-prepared French mustard with the cornflour and apple juice.

French Fondue with Garlic Sausage

Make as French Fondue in Swiss Mood, adding 2 oz (50 g) finely chopped fresh garlic sausage with the cornflour and apple juice.

French Fondue with Tarragon

Make as French Fondue in Swiss Mood, adding 2 tablespoons finely chopped fresh tarragon before serving.

French Fondue with Pink Peppercorns

Make as French Fondue in Swiss Mood, adding 2–3 teaspoons coarsely ground pink peppercorns before serving.

CAMEMBERT CREAM FONDUE

With all the style in the world, this is a gourmet fondue with a haute cuisine label. Quite outstanding with cubes of very fresh baguette or crusty rolls, a must for entertaining. Keep the Camembert in the refrigerator until the last minute.

SERVES 4

8 fl. oz (225 ml) sparkling white wine
9 oz (250 g) Camembert, de-rinded and finely grated
8 oz (225 g) Emmental cheese, de-rinded and finely grated
1 teaspoon lemon juice
3½ level teaspoons cornflour
2 fl. oz (50 ml) single cream
3 teaspoons Armagnac

FOR DIPPING
cubes of crusty French bread or rolls

1. Pour the wine into the fondue pot and heat until hot. Add the cheeses and lemon juice.

2. Cook over a medium heat, stirring all the time, until mixture just begins to bubble.

3. Blend the cornflour to a thinnish paste with the cream and add to the cheese mixture.

4. Cook slowly, still stirring, until the mixture comes to the boil and thickens to a smooth and creamy consistency. Do not over-boil or it may become stringy. Stir in the Armagnac.

5. Stand the fondue pot over a spirit stove and eat straight away with cubes of crusty bread.

HIGH-SPIRITED FRENCH FONDUE

Quite a mix, this one, and designed for devotees of pastis, be it Pernod or Ricard. Keep both cheeses in the refrigerator until you are ready to use them as this makes grating easier. Flavour? Herby and spicy at the same time.

SERVES 4

9 fl. oz (250 ml) white vermouth
8 oz (225 g) Tomme de Savoie cheese, de-rinded and finely grated
8 oz (225 g) Port Salut cheese, de-rinded and finely grated
1 teaspoon lemon juice
1 level tablespoon cornflour
2 tablespoons Pernod

FOR DIPPING
cubes of brown bread or homemade Mustard Bread (page 25)
cubes of freshly boiled potatoes or whole new potatoes

1. Pour the vermouth into the fondue pot and heat until hot. Mix in the cheeses and lemon juice.

2. Cook over a medium heat, stirring all the time, until the cheeses melt and the mixture just begins to bubble.

3. Blend the cornflour to a thin paste with the Pernod and add to the cheese mixture.

4. Cook slowly, still stirring, until the mixture comes to the boil and thickens to a smooth and creamy consistency. Do not over-boil or it may become stringy.

5. Stand the fondue pot over a spirit stove and eat straight away with cubes of brown bread and/or chunks of freshly boiled potatoes.

TRUE BLUE BRITISH FONDUE

Why not be different and serve this fondue *after* dinner, instead of cheese and biscuits? With 'dippers' of celery pieces and cubes of brown bread, it reflects faithfully our love of Port, Stilton and Cheddar and would be an unusual way of rounding off a special lunch or dinner. Or just keep the fondue as a main meal.

SERVES 4–8

4 fl. oz (100 ml) English white wine
¼ pint (150 ml) port
5 oz (150 g) Stilton cheese, de-rinded and crumbled
11 oz (300 g) mature Cheddar cheese, de-rinded and finely grated
1 teaspoon lemon juice
1 level tablespoon cornflour

FOR DIPPING
pieces of celery
cubes of brown bread or homemade Anchovy and Chive Bread (page 25)

1. Pour the wine and 4 fl. oz (120 ml) of the port into the fondue pot and heat until hot. Mix in the grated cheeses and lemon juice.

2. Cook over a medium heat, stirring all the time, until the cheeses melt and the mixture just begins to bubble.

3. Blend the cornflour to a thin paste with the remaining 1 fl. oz (25 ml) of port, and add to the cheese mixture.

4. Cook slowly, still stirring, until the mixture comes to the boil and thickens to a smooth and creamy consistency. Do not over-boil or it may become stringy.

5. Stand the fondue pot over a spirit stove and eat straight away with pieces of celery or brown bread.

True Blue British Fondue with Whisky
Make as above but use whisky instead of port.

ENGLISH MIXED-BAG FONDUE

Practical for using up spare cheeses and quite zippy with its White Stilton and brandy. Eat with cubes of fruit or seed bread or try apple and banana chunks.

SERVES 4

8 fl. oz (225 ml) white wine
9 oz (250 g) White Stilton, de-rinded (if necessary) and crumbled
*7 oz (200 g) mix of any English cheeses such as Cheddar, Wensley-
dale, Derby, Red Leicester, etc., de-rinded and finely grated.*
1 teaspoon lemon juice
1 level tablespoon cornflour
1 fl. oz (25 ml) brandy

FOR DIPPING
cubes of fruit bread or homemade Mixed Seed Bread (page 26)
chunks of apple, peeled
chunks of banana

1. Pour the wine into the fondue pot and heat until hot. Add the grated cheeses and lemon juice.

2. Cook over a medium heat, stirring all the time, until the cheeses melt and the mixture just begins to bubble.

3. Blend the cornflour to a thin paste with the brandy and add to the cheese mixture.

4. Cook slowly, still stirring, until the mixture comes to the boil and thickens to a smooth and creamy consistency. Do not over-boil or it may become stringy.

5. Stand the fondue pot over a spirit stove and eat straight away with a selection of dippers.

PLOUGHMAN'S LUNCH FONDUE

*T*ingling with perry (pear cider) and its taste sharpened with pickled onions, this lively fondue resembles a make-at-home pub lunch with extra style. Try it sometime for Sunday lunch.

SERVES 4

8 fl. oz (225 ml) sparkling perry
1 lb (450 g) Cheddar cheese, de-rinded and finely grated
1 teaspoon lemon juice
1 level teaspoon English mustard powder
1 level tablespoon cornflour
2 fl. oz (50 ml) milk
4 vinegar-pickled brown onions, drained and finely chopped

FOR DIPPING
cubes of coarse-grained brown bread

1. Pour the perry into the fondue pot and heat until hot. Mix in the grated cheese and lemon juice.

2. Cook over a medium heat, stirring all the time, until the cheese melts and the mixture just begins to bubble.

3. Blend the mustard powder and cornflour to a thin paste with the milk and add to the cheese mixture.

4. Cook slowly, still stirring, until the mixture comes to the boil and thickens to a smooth and creamy consistency. Do not over-boil or it may become stringy. Stir in the chopped onion.

5. Stand the fondue pot over a spirit stove and eat straight away with cubes of coarse-grained brown bread.

Pepperpot Fondue
Make as above, omitting the mustard, and adding 1–2 teaspoons freshly ground black pepper after the fondue has thickened.

Black Walnut Fondue
Make as Ploughman's Lunch Fondue, omitting the pickled onions and substituting 3 chopped pickled walnuts.

Colonial Fondue

Make as Ploughman's Lunch Fondue, omitting the pickled onions and substituting 2 tablespoons chutney (smooth rather than chunky). If liked, also add 2 level teaspoons medium curry powder instead of the mustard and add at the same time as the chutney.

Saucy Fondue

Make as Ploughman's Lunch Fondue, omitting the pickled onions and substituting 3 tablespoons of brown ketchup.

Gherkin Fondue

Make as Ploughman's Lunch Fondue, omitting the pickled onions and substituting 2 tablespoons finely chopped gherkins.

BLOODY MARY FONDUE

Glowing golden orange like a summer sunset, this is a stunningly tasty fondue flavoured, cocktail style, with tomato and Worcestershire sauce.

SERVES 4

1 garlic clove, peeled and halved
8 fl. oz (225 ml) white wine
1 lb (450 g) Cheddar cheese, de-rinded and finely grated
1 teaspoon lemon juice
1 level tablespoon cornflour
1 fl. oz (25 ml) vodka
2 tablespoons tomato ketchup
1 teaspoon Worcestershire sauce

FOR DIPPING
pieces of celery
squares of green pepper
cubes of homemade Onion Bread (page 26)

1. Rub the cut sides of garlic over the base and sides of the fondue pot.

2. Pour in the white wine and heat until hot. Mix in the grated cheese and lemon juice.

3. Cook over a medium heat, stirring all the time, until the cheese melts and the mixture just begins to bubble.

4. Blend the cornflour to a thin paste with the vodka. Add to the cheese mixture, together with the tomato ketchup and Worcestershire sauce.

5. Cook slowly, still stirring, until the mixture comes to the boil and thickens to a smooth and creamy consistency. Do not overboil or it may become stringy.

6. Stand the fondue pot over a spirit stove and eat straight away with 'dippers' of celery, green pepper and white bread.

TROPICAL FONDUE

*M*ade with crushed pineapple and spiked with orange liqueur, this is a most unusual sweet-sour fondue which is absolutely delicious with cubes of fruit bread or spicy fruit buns.

SERVES 4–6

1 lb (450 g) Cheddar cheese, de-rinded and finely grated
one 15 oz (432 g) can crushed pineapple in its own juice
6 fl. oz (175 ml) white wine
1 level tablespoon cornflour
2 fl. oz (50 ml) orange or mandarin liqueur

FOR DIPPING
cubes of fruit bread or homemade Orange and Date Bread (page 25)
pieces of spicy fruit buns

1. Put the grated cheese into the fondue pot with the crushed pineapple, its juice and the wine.

2. Cook over a medium heat, stirring all the time, until the cheese melts and the mixture just begins to bubble.

3. Blend the cornflour to a thin paste with the liqueur and add to the cheese mixture.

4. Cook slowly, still stirring, until the mixture comes to the boil and thickens to a creamy consistency — it won't be as smooth as other fondues because of the pineapple. Do not over-boil or it may become stringy.

5. Stand the fondue pot over a spirit stove and eat straight away with cubes of fruit bread or spicy fruit buns.

Tropical Fondue with Coconut
Make as above, adding 1 level tablespoon toasted coconut to the cheese mixture with the cornflour paste.

Tropical Fondue with Melon Liqueur
Make as Tropical Fondue, substituting 2 fl. oz (50 ml) Midori (a green, melon-flavoured liqueur) for the orange liqueur.

SMOKY APPLE FONDUE

*S*moky Applewood cheese and fresh White Stilton make this the queen of fondues. It is absolutely glorious and no words of mine can do full justice to its quality, so try it and see for yourself.

SERVES 4

9 fl. oz (250 ml) low-alcohol cider
9 oz (250 g) Ilchester Applewood cheese, finely grated (including rind)
7 oz (200 g) White Stilton, de-rinded (if necessary) and crumbled
1 teaspoon lemon juice
1 level tablespoon cornflour

FOR DIPPING
cubes of wholemeal bread

1. Pour 8 fl. oz (225 ml) of the cider into the fondue pot and heat until hot. Mix in the grated cheeses and lemon juice.

2. Cook over a medium heat, stirring all the time, until the cheeses melt and the mixture just begins to bubble.

3. Blend the cornflour to a thin paste with the remaining 1 fl. oz (25 ml) cider, and add to the cheese mixture.

4. Cook slowly, still stirring, until the mixture comes to the boil and thickens to a smooth and creamy consistency. Do not over-boil or it may become stringy.

5. Stand the fondue pot over a spirit stove and eat straight away with cubes of wholemeal bread.

BACHELORS' PARTY FONDUE

Headstrong and with a distinctive bitter after-taste, this is one for the boys and can be swished down with ale and served with chunks of French bread. It's Andy Capp territory!

SERVES 4

9 fl. oz (250 ml) pale ale
8 oz (225 g) White Cheshire cheese, de-rinded and finely grated
8 oz (225 g) Derby cheese, de-rinded and finely grated
1 teaspoon lemon juice
4 level tablespoons cornflour

FOR DIPPING
cubes of crusty French bread or homemade Oriental Bread (page 25)

1. Pour 8 fl. oz (225 ml) of the ale into the fondue pot and heat until hot. Mix in the grated cheeses and lemon juice.

2. Cook over a medium heat, stirring all the time, until the cheeses melt and the mixture just begins to bubble.

3. Blend the cornflour to a thin paste with the remaining 1 fl. oz (25 ml) ale, and add to the cheese mixture.

4. Cook slowly, still stirring, until the mixture comes to the boil and thickens to a smooth and creamy consistency. Do not over-boil or it may become stringy.

5. Stand the fondue pot over a spirit stove and eat straight away with cubes of crusty French bread.

Bachelors' Spicy Party Fondue

Make as above, but add 2 teaspoons Worcestershire sauce and 5 drops Tabasco sauce after the fondue has thickened. Stir in well.

THOROUGHBRED ENGLISH FONDUE

Made with some of the best of our traditional cheeses, this comes up trumps every time and is a warm gold with a beautiful taste. Serve with diced-up crusty rolls.

SERVES 4

9 fl. oz (250 ml) vintage cider
7 oz (200 g) Blue Cheshire cheese, de-rinded and crumbled
7 oz (200 g) Double Gloucester cheese, de-rinded and finely grated
2 oz (50 g) Red Leicester cheese, de-rinded and finely grated
1 teaspoon lemon juice
1 level tablespoon cornflour

FOR DIPPING
pieces of crusty bread rolls or homemade Onion Bread (page 26)

1. Pour 8 fl. oz (225 ml) of the cider into the fondue pot and heat until hot. Mix in the grated cheeses and lemon juice.

2. Cook over a medium heat, stirring all the time, until the cheeses melt and the mixture just begins to bubble.

3. Blend the cornflour to a thin paste with the remaining 1 fl. oz (25 ml) of cider and add to the cheese mixture.

4. Cook slowly, still stirring, until the mixture comes to the boil and thickens to a smooth and creamy consistency. Do not over-boil or it may become stringy.

5. Stand the fondue pot over a spirit stove and eat straight away with pieces of crusty rolls.

Thoroughbred English Fondue with Peanuts

Make as above but add 1 oz (25 g) very finely chopped salted peanuts after fondue has thickened. Mix in well.

RIGHT: *The Bread Basket (see pages: 23–6)*

FONDUE FROM THE ENGLISH SHIRES

*D*eep orange in colour and as smooth as silk, this fondue has a hearty and distinguished flavour. Eat with pieces of freshly toasted muffins or teacakes.

SERVES 4

8 fl. oz (225 ml) pale ale
10 oz (275 g) Farmhouse Red Leicester cheese, de-rinded and finely grated
6 oz (175 g) Farmhouse Wensleydale cheese, de-rinded and finely grated
1 teaspoon lemon juice
1 level tablespoon cornflour
1 fl. oz (25 ml) water
1 teaspoon prepared English mustard

FOR DIPPING
pieces of freshly toasted muffins or teacakes

1. Pour the ale into the fondue pot and heat until hot. Add the grated cheeses and lemon juice.

2. Cook over a medium heat, stirring all the time, until the cheeses melt and the mixture just begins to bubble.

3. Blend the cornflour to a thin paste with the water and add to the cheese mixture.

4. Cook slowly, still stirring, until the mixture comes to the boil and thickens to a smooth and creamy consistency. Do not over-boil or it may become stringy.

5. Stand the fondue pot over a spirit stove and eat straight away with pieces of toasted muffin or teacake.

LEFT: *Swiss Cheese Fondue (see pages 32–3)*

COUNTRYSIDE COMPANION FONDUE

A warm-tasting, golden-hued fondue, laced with vintage cider and brown pickle. Eat with wedges of chicken or turkey breast, chipolata sausages or large prawns.

SERVES 4

8 fl. oz (225 ml) vintage cider
1 lb (450 g) Double Gloucester cheese, de-rinded and finely grated
1 teaspoon lemon juice
1 level tablespoon cornflour
1 fl. oz (25 ml) milk
2 tablespoons brown pickle

FOR DIPPING
wedges of cooked chicken or turkey breast
pieces of cooked chipolata sausages
large prawns, shelled

1. Pour the cider into the fondue pot and heat until hot. Mix in the grated cheese and lemon juice.

2. Cook over a medium heat, stirring all the time, until the cheese melts and the mixture just begins to bubble.

3. Blend the cornflour to a thin paste with the milk and add to the cheese mixture with the pickle.

4. Cook slowly, still stirring, until the mixture comes to the boil and thickens to a smooth and creamy consistency. Do not over-boil or it may become stringy.

5. Stand the fondue pot over a spirit stove and eat straight away with your choice of 'dippers'.

Countryside Fondue with a Touch of Brown
Make as above, substituting 3 tablespoons of brown ketchup for the pickle.

LANCASHIRE FONDUE WITH BITE

A sharpish lass here, tangy with cider and brown vinegar from a jar of pickled onions. The Lancashire cheese adds its own note of distinction and the 'dippers' should be on the sweet side, such as thickish slices of apple, quarters of firm pear, wedges of currant buns, even dried apricots soaked overnight in water and thoroughly drained.

SERVES 4

8 fl. oz (225 ml) medium dry cider
1 lb (450 g) Lancashire cheese, de-rinded and crumbled
1 level tablespoon cornflour
1 tablespoon brown vinegar from a jar of pickled onions
Freshly ground black pepper, to taste

FOR DIPPING
thick apple slices, peeled
quarters of firm pears, peeled
wedges of currant buns
dried apricots, soaked in water overnight and thoroughly drained

1. Pour the cider into the fondue pot and heat until hot. Mix in the crumbled cheese.

2. Cook over a medium heat, stirring all the time, until the cheese melts and the mixture just begins to bubble.

3. Blend the cornflour to a thin paste with the vinegar and add to the cheese mixture with black pepper to taste.

4. Cook slowly, still stirring, until the mixture comes to the boil and thickens to a smooth and creamy consistency. Do not over-boil or it may become stringy.

5. Stand the fondue pot over a spirit stove and eat straight away with a selection of the 'dippers' given above.

Lancashire Walnut Fondue
Make as above, adding 1 oz (25 g) finely chopped walnuts with the cornflour and vinegar.

WEST COUNTRY FONDUE

Made from 3 notable English cheeses plus a dash of vintage cider, this is a classy tasting fondue with delicacy. Eat with cubes of brown bread and pieces of freshly toasted crumpet.

SERVES 4

8 fl. oz (225 ml) milk
5 oz (150 g) Creamy White Lymeswold cheese, de-rinded and cut into pieces
5 oz (150 g) Lymeswold English County Brie, de-rinded and cut into pieces
7 oz (200 g) Cheddar cheese, de-rinded and finely grated
4 level teaspoons cornflour
1 fl. oz (25 ml) vintage cider

FOR DIPPING
cubes of brown bread
pieces of freshly toasted crumpets

1. Heat the milk in the fondue pot until hot. Mix in the cheeses.

2. Cook over a medium heat, stirring all the time, until the cheeses melt and the mixture just begins to bubble.

3. Blend the cornflour to a thin paste with the cider and add to the cheese mixture.

4. Cook slowly, still stirring, until the mixture comes to the boil and thickens to a smooth and creamy consistency. Do not over-boil or it may become stringy.

5. Stand the fondue pot over a spirit stove and eat straight away with cubes of brown bread or pieces of crumpet.

West Country Fondue with Anchovy

Make as above, adding $\frac{1}{2}$–1 teaspoon anchovy essence to the thickened fondue. Stir well.

OLD-ENGLISH FONDUE WITH GINGER

With old-English flavours and based on Sage Derby and White Cheshire cheeses, this is a triumph of a fondue in elegant green with a distinctive fragrance and slight gingery aroma.

SERVES 4

8 fl. oz (225 ml) perry (pear cider)
10 oz (275 g) Sage Derby cheese, de-rinded and finely grated
6 oz (175 g) White Cheshire, de-rinded and finely grated
1 teaspoon lemon juice
1 level tablespoon cornflour
1 fl. oz (25 ml) ginger wine

FOR DIPPING
cubes of homemade Hazelnut and Nutmeg Bread (page 25)

1. Heat the perry in the fondue pot until hot. Mix in the grated cheeses and lemon juice.

2. Cook over a medium heat, stirring all the time, until the cheeses melt and the mixture just begins to bubble.

3. Blend the cornflour to a thin paste with the wine and add to the cheese mixture.

4. Cook slowly, still stirring, until the mixture comes to the boil and thickens to a smooth and creamy consistency. Do not over-boil or it may become stringy.

5. Stand the fondue pot over a spirit stove and eat straight away with cubes of Hazelnut and Nutmeg Bread.

Extra Green Fondue
Make as above, stirring in 2 level tablespoons finely chopped parsley just before serving.

WHISKY-MAC CHEDDAR FONDUE

*P*acked with flavour and predictably potent, this is the fondue to eat after a day on the ski slopes of Scotland. It's a marvellous insulator and with tots of whisky is guaranteed to make any evening a lively and entertaining occasion.

SERVES 4

7 fl. oz (200 ml) stout
1 lb (450 g) mature Cheddar cheese, de-rinded and finely grated
1 teaspoon lemon juice
1 level tablespoon cornflour
2 fl. oz (50 ml) whisky

FOR DIPPING
cubes of homemade Chilli Bread (page 25)

1. Pour the stout into the fondue pot and heat until hot. Mix in the grated cheese and lemon juice.

2. Cook over a medium heat, stirring all the time, until the cheese melts and the mixture just begins to bubble.

3. Blend the cornflour to a thin paste with the whisky and add to the cheese mixture.

4. Cook slowly, still stirring, until the mixture comes to the boil and thickens to a smooth and creamy consistency. Do not over-boil or it may become stringy.

5. Stand the fondue pot over a spirit stove and eat straight away with cubes of homemade Chilli Bread.

Highland Drambuie Fondue
Make as above, substituting Drambuie for the whisky. Although Drambuie is sweet, it partially counteracts the bitterness of the stout and so makes the fondue pleasingly mellow.

Blarney Fondue

With all Irish produce and whiskey spelled with an 'e', this goes down a treat with Irish soda bread or cubes of wholemeal, hot new potatoes and Dublin Bay prawns.

Serves 4

8 fl. oz (225 ml) Guinness
1 lb (450 g) Irish Cheddar cheese, de-rinded and finely grated
1 level tablespoon cornflour
2 fl. oz (50 ml) Irish whiskey

For Dipping
cubes of soda bread
cubes of wholemeal bread
hot new potatoes
Dublin Bay prawns, peeled

1. Pour the Guinness into the fondue pot and heat until hot. Mix in the grated cheese.

2. Cook over a medium heat, stirring all the time, until the cheese melts and the mixture just begins to bubble.

3. Blend the cornflour to a thin paste with the whiskey and add to the cheese mixture.

4. Cook slowly, still stirring, until the mixture comes to the boil and thickens to a smooth and creamy consistency. Do not over-boil as it may become stringy.

5. Stand the fondue pot over a spirit stove and eat straight away with a selection of 'dippers'.

Blarney Fondue with Crab

Make as above, adding 2 oz (50 g) cooked crabmeat to the fondue at the same time as the cornflour and whiskey.

ITALIAN MYSTERY FONDUE

The mystery of this one lies in its unique flavour brought about by the addition of golden Galliano. And its power. It is definitely a cheese-lover's fantasy and is another one that can be served confidently at the end of a meal instead of cheese and biscuits.

SERVES 4

8 fl. oz (225 ml) white wine
10 oz (275 g) Gorgonzola cheese, de-rinded and crumbled
6 oz (175 g) Parmesan cheese, de-rinded and grated
1 level tablespoon cornflour
2 fl. oz (50 ml) Galliano

FOR DIPPING
cubes of homemade Anchovy and Chive Bread (page 25)
cubes of mild-flavoured ham
pieces of cooked fennel
halved artichoke hearts

1. Pour the wine into the fondue pot and heat until hot. Mix in the grated cheeses.

2. Cook over a medium heat, stirring all the time, until the cheeses melt and the mixture just begins to bubble.

3. Blend the cornflour to a thin paste with the Galliano and add to the cheese mixture.

4. Cook slowly, still stirring, until the mixture comes to the boil and thickens to a smooth and creamy consistency. Do not over-boil or it may become stringy.

5. Stand the fondue pot over a spirit stove and eat straight away with a selection of 'dippers'.

Italian Mystery Fondue with Basil
Make as Italian Mystery Fondue, adding 2 level tablespoons very finely chopped fresh basil to the thickened fondue.

Italian Fondue with Asti Spumante

A joyous fondue, bubbling with Asti Spumante in true Italian style. It is made with two of Italy's best-loved cheeses: mild Bel Paese (which means beautiful country) and piquant Provolone. Eat with pieces of crusty white bread or even Grissini sticks.

Serves 4

8 fl. oz (225 ml) Asti Spumante
10 oz (275 g) Provolone cheese, de-rinded and finely grated
6 oz (175 g) Bel Paese cheese, de-rinded and finely grated
1 teaspoon lemon juice
1 level tablespoon cornflour
2 fl. oz (50 ml) Marsala

For Dipping
cubes of homemade Italian Bread (page 25)
Grissini sticks

1. Pour the Asti Spumante into the fondue pot and heat until hot. Add the grated cheeses and lemon juice.

2. Cook over a medium heat, stirring all the time, until the cheeses melt and the mixture just begins to bubble.

3. Blend the cornflour to a thin paste with the Marsala and add to the cheese mixture.

4. Cook slowly, still stirring, until the mixture comes to the boil and thickens to a smooth and creamy consistency. Do not over-boil or it may become stringy.

5. Stand the fondue pot over a spirit stove and eat straight away with cubes of Italian bread or Grissini sticks.

Italian Fondue with Asti Spumante and Garlic

Make as above, but add 1 peeled and crushed garlic clove at the same time as the cheese and lemon juice.

DANISH RUM FONDUE

Designed for a Scandinavian winter, this fondue takes the chill from the heart and will leave you glowing and comforted.

SERVES 4

7 fl. oz (200 ml) white wine
8 oz (225 g) Esrom cheese, de-rinded and finely grated
8 oz (225 g) Danbo cheese, de-rinded and finely grated
1 teaspoon lemon juice
1 level tablespoon cornflour
2 fl. oz (50 ml) rum

FOR DIPPING
cubes of dark rye bread

1. Pour the wine into the fondue pot and heat until hot. Add the cheeses and lemon juice.

2. Cook over a medium heat, stirring all the time, until the cheeses melt and the mixture just begins to bubble.

3. Blend the cornflour to a thin paste with the rum and add to the cheese mixture.

4. Cook slowly, still stirring, until the mixture comes to the boil and thickens to a smooth and creamy consistency. Do not over-boil or it may become stringy.

5. Stand the fondue pot over a spirit stove and eat straight away with cubes of dark rye bread.

Danish Devil Fondue

Make as above, adding 1 teaspoon Worcestershire sauce, 1 peeled and crushed garlic clove and 4 drops Tabasco sauce with the lemon juice.

DANISH DE-LUXE FONDUE

A good one this, enhanced with French mustard and dill pepper. Eat with crisp-crusted bread cubes or pieces of roll.

SERVES 4

8 fl. oz (225 ml) white wine
1 lb (450 g) Havarti cheese, de-rinded and finely grated
1 teaspoon French mustard
1 level tablespoon cornflour
2 fl. oz (50 ml) kirsch
dill pepper, to taste

FOR DIPPING
cubes of homemade Spicy Bread (page 25)

1. Pour the wine into the fondue pot and heat until hot. Mix in the grated cheese and mustard.

2. Cook over a medium heat, stirring all the time, until the cheese melts and the mixture just begins to bubble.

3. Blend the cornflour to a thin paste with the kirsch and add to the cheese mixture. Cover the surface with a sprinkling of dill pepper.

4. Cook slowly, still stirring, until the mixture comes to the boil and thickens to a smooth and creamy consistency. Do not over-boil or it may become stringy.

5. Stand the fondue pot over a spirit stove and eat straight away with pieces of crusty bread.

Danish De-Luxe Fondue with Bacon
Make as above, adding 2 oz (50 g) finely chopped boiled Danish bacon to the thickened fondue.

Danish De-Luxe Fondue with Chives
Make as Danish De-Luxe Fondue, adding 3 tablespoons finely chopped fresh chives to the thickened fondue.

GREAT DANE FONDUE

This is a hearty, cold-weather fondue with plenty of good flavour.

SERVES 4

8 fl. oz (225 ml) Danish lager
8 oz (225 g) Havarti cheese, de-rinded and finely grated
8 oz (225 g) Samsø cheese, de-rinded and finely grated
1 teaspoon lemon juice
¼ teaspoon caraway seeds
4 level teaspoons cornflour
2 fl. oz (50 ml) schnapps (German korn or Dutch gin fit well)

FOR DIPPING
cubes of Danish salami
cubes of ham
cubes of rye bread

1. Pour the lager into the fondue pot and heat until hot. Mix in the cheeses, lemon juice and caraway seeds.

2. Cook over a medium heat, stirring all the time, until the cheeses melt and the mixture just begins to bubble.

3. Blend the cornflour to a thin paste with the schnapps and add to the cheese mixture.

4. Cook slowly, still stirring, until the mixture comes to the boil and thickens to a smooth and creamy consistency. Do not over-boil or it may become stringy.

5. Stand the fondue pot over a spirit stove. Eat straight away with cubes of salami, ham and rye bread.

Timid Great Dane Fondue
For a gentler version of the above fondue, use a low-alcohol lager and mix the cornflour with water instead of schnapps.

HALF AND HALF FONDUE

Made half with blue cheese and half with white this is strong, buxom and on the salty side. Delicacy is not the hallmark of this Scandinavian fondue, so make it only if you like strong and potent cheeses.

SERVES 4

8 fl. oz (225 ml) white wine
4 oz (125 g) Mycella cheese, de-rinded and crumbled
4 oz (125 g) Danish Blue cheese, de-rinded and crumbled
8 oz (225 g) Svenbo cheese, de-rinded and finely grated
1 teaspoon lemon juice
1 garlic clove, peeled and crushed
1 level tablespoon cornflour
2 fl. oz (50 ml) gin

FOR DIPPING
cubes of soft white bread

1. Pour the wine into the fondue pot and heat until hot. Mix in the grated cheeses, lemon juice and garlic.

2. Cook over a medium heat, stirring all the time, until the cheeses melt and the mixture just begins to bubble.

3. Blend the cornflour to a thin paste with the gin and add to the cheese mixture.

4. Cook slowly, still stirring, until the mixture comes to the boil and thickens to a smooth and creamy consistency. Do not over-boil or it may become stringy.

5. Stand the fondue pot over a spirit stove and eat straight away with cubes of soft white bread.

COPENHAGENER FONDUE

*T*his is quite a strong fondue with a subtle hint of blue from the Mycella cheese. Serve with prawns, Danish salami, cubes of dark rye bread, freshly cooked new potatoes with or without their skins and fingers of fresh pineapple.

SERVES 4

8 fl. oz (225 ml) dry white wine
8 oz (225 g) Havarti cheese, de-rinded and finely grated
4 oz (125 g) Svenbo cheese, de-rinded and finely grated
4 oz (125 g) Mycella cheese, de-rinded and crumbled
2 teaspoons horseradish sauce
1 teaspoon lemon juice
1 level tablespoon cornflour
1 fl. oz (25 ml) Linie Aquavit or gin

FOR DIPPING
peeled prawns
cubes of Danish salami
cubes of dark rye bread
new potatoes
fingers of fresh pineapple

1. Pour the wine into the fondue pot and heat until hot. Mix in the grated cheeses, horseradish sauce and lemon juice.

2. Cook over a medium heat, stirring all the time, until the cheeses melt and the mixture just begins to bubble.

3. Blend the cornflour to a thin paste with the Linie Aquavit or gin and add to the cheese mixture.

4. Cook slowly, still stirring, until the mixture comes to the boil and thickens to a smooth and creamy consistency. Do not over-boil or it may become stringy.

5. Stand the fondue pot over a spirit stove and eat straight away with a selection of 'dippers'.

Copenhagener Fondue with Capers

Make as Copenhagener Fondue, adding 1 tablespoon drained and chopped capers at the same time as the horseradish sauce.

Copenhagener Fondue with Fish

Make as Copenhagener Fondue, adding 2 oz (50 g) finely mashed fresh or smoked fish at the same time as the horseradish sauce.

NORWEGIAN FONDUE WITH KICK

Laced with Norway's Linie Aquavit and German Holsten Pils lager, this is strong stuff for stout stomachs and a tribute to three of Norway's best-loved cheeses: Ridder, Jarlsberg and Gjetost. Suitable for special occasions.

SERVES 4

8 fl. oz (225 ml) Holsten Pils lager
10 oz (275 g) Ridder cheese, de-rinded and finely grated
4 oz (125 g) Jarlsberg cheese, de-rinded and finely grated
2 oz (50 g) Gjetost cheese, de-rinded and finely grated
1 teaspoon lemon juice
1 level tablespoon cornflour
1 fl. oz (25 ml) Linie Aquavit or any other aquavit available.

FOR DIPPING
cubes of homemade Oriental Bread (page 25)
pieces of grilled or fried sausages

1. Heat the lager in the fondue pot until hot. Add the grated cheeses and lemon juice.

2. Cook over a medium heat, stirring all the time, until the cheeses melt and the mixture just begins to bubble.

3. Mix the cornflour to a thin paste with the Aquavit and add to the cheese mixture.

4. Cook slowly, still stirring, until the mixture comes to the boil and thickens to a smooth and creamy consistency. Do not over-boil or it may become stringy.

5. Stand the fondue pot over a spirit stove and eat straight away with cubes of bread and/or pieces of grilled or fried sausages.

Norwegian Fondue with Fennel
Make as above, adding 1 tablespoon chopped fresh fennel fronds before adding the cornflour paste.

RIGHT: *Greek Retreat Fondue (see page 67)*

DUTCH FONDUE WITH BACON

A winning two-cheese fondue freckled with bacon – a comely meal, eaten with hot, cubed potatoes or brown bread.

SERVES 4

4 oz (125 g) lean, unsmoked bacon, finely chopped
8 fl. oz (225 ml) white wine
8 oz (225 g) Gouda cheese, de-rinded and finely chopped
8 oz (225 g) Edam cheese, de-rinded and finely chopped
1 teaspoon lemon juice
2½ level teaspoons cornflour
2 fl. oz (50 ml) kirsch, gin or vodka

FOR DIPPING
pieces of hot potatoes
cubes of brown bread

1. Slowly fry or grill the bacon until crisp.

2. Pour the wine into the fondue pot and heat until hot. Add the chopped cheese and lemon juice.

3. Cook over a medium heat, stirring all the time, until the cheese melts and the mixture just begins to bubble.

4. Blend the cornflour to a thin paste with the kirsch, gin or vodka. Add to the cheese mixture with the cooked bacon.

5. Cook slowly, still stirring, until the mixture comes to the boil and thickens to a smooth and creamy consistency. Do not over-boil or it may become stringy.

6. Stand the fondue pot over a spirit stove and eat straight away with pieces of potato or brown bread.

Dutch Fondue with Pickled Cucumber
Make as above, substituting 3 tablespoons finely chopped pickled cucumber for the bacon.

LEFT: *Ploughman's Lunch Fondue (see page 42)*

GOUDA FONDUE

Golden cream in colour, smooth, delicious and laced with powerful Genever gin, this is a truly Dutch special. In the absence of Genever gin, use ordinary.

SERVES 4

8 fl. oz (225 ml) white wine
1 lb (450 g) Gouda cheese, de-rinded and finely grated
1 teaspoon lemon juice
2½ level teaspoons cornflour
2 fl. oz (50 ml) Genever gin

FOR DIPPING
cubes of brown bread

1. Pour the wine into the fondue pot and heat until hot. Add the grated cheese and lemon juice.

2. Cook over a medium heat, stirring all the time, until the cheese melts and the mixture just begins to bubble.

3. Blend the cornflour to a thin paste with the gin and add to the cheese mixture.

4. Cook slowly, still stirring, until the mixture comes to the boil and thickens to a smooth and creamy consistency. Do not over-boil or it may become stringy.

5. Stand the fondue pot over a spirit stove and eat straight away with cubes of brown bread.

Gouda Fondue with Egg
Make as above, adding 1 finely chopped hard-boiled egg to the thickened fondue.

Gouda Fondue with Capers
Make as Gouda Fondue, adding 1 tablespoon drained and finely chopped capers to the thickened fondue.

GREEK RETREAT FONDUE

With happy memories of lazy holidays on Greek islands and with all those typical taverna flavours coming from the traditional sheep's milk cheeses, olive oil and ouzo, this is essentially a summer fondue for eating outdoors. I set up the spirit stove in the garden and dip in cubes of homemade Sesame and Fennel Seed Bread — heaven. Don't be tempted to use wine instead of milk as it disagrees with these particular cheeses and will turn them into a rubbery ball sitting in a pool of liquid.

SERVES 4

8 fl. oz (225 ml) milk
9 oz (250 g) Halloumi cheese, de-rinded and finely grated
7 oz (200 g) Feta cheese, crumbled
1 level tablespoon cornflour
1 fl. oz (25 ml) water
2 teaspoons olive oil
1 teaspoon ouzo or 2 teaspoons brandy

FOR DIPPING
cubes of homemade Sesame and Fennel Seed Bread (page 25)

1. Pour the milk into the fondue pot and heat until hot. Mix in the grated cheeses.

2. Cook over a medium heat, stirring all the time, until the cheeses melt and the mixture just begins to bubble.

3. Blend the cornflour to a thin paste with the water and add to the cheese mixture.

4. Cook slowly, still stirring, until the mixture comes to the boil and thickens to a smooth and creamy consistency. Do not over-boil or it may become stringy.

5. Stir in the oil and ouzo.

6. Stand the fondue pot over a spirit stove and eat straight away with cubes of Sesame and Fennel Seed Bread.

MEXICAN CHILLI FONDUE

*H*ot, hot, hot or as mild as you like, this is a real cracker of a fondue which can be eaten with 'dippers' of Taco chips or cubes of white bread. It is bright orange in colour and uses Tequila, Mexico's national firewater.

SERVES 4

8 fl. oz (225 ml) lager or white wine
8 oz (225 g) Cheddar cheese, de-rinded and finely grated
8 oz (225 g) Red Leicester cheese, de-rinded and finely grated
1 teaspoon lemon juice
1 level teaspoon mild chilli seasoning
1 level tablespoon cornflour
1 fl. oz (25 ml) Tequila

FOR DIPPING
Taco chips
cubes of crusty white bread

1. Pour the wine or lager into the fondue pot and heat until hot. Add the grated cheeses and lemon juice.

2. Cook over a medium heat, stirring all the time, until the cheeses melt and the mixture just begins to bubble.

3. Blend the chilli seasoning and cornflour to a thin paste with the Tequila and add to the cheese mixture.

4. Cook slowly, still stirring, until the mixture comes to the boil and thickens to a smooth and creamy consistency. Do not over-boil or it may become stringy.

5. Stand the fondue pot over a spirit stove and eat straight away with Taco chips or cubes of white bread.

Mexican Chilli Fondue with Mashed Beans
Make as Mexican Chilli Fondue, adding 3 tablespoons mashed red kidney beans to the thickened fondue. Use canned cooked beans that have been well drained.

DOWN-UNDER FONDUE

A fondue dedicated to all Australians and spiced with Vegemite, their national spread.

SERVES 4

9 fl. oz (250 ml) lager
11 oz (300 g) strong Australian Cheddar cheese, de-rinded and finely grated
5 oz (150 g) Emmental cheese, de-rinded and finely grated
1 teaspoon lemon juice
1 level tablespoon cornflour
2 teaspoons Vegemite

FOR DIPPING
cubes of homemade Mixed Seed Bread (page 26)

1. Pour 8 fl. oz (225 ml) of the lager into the fondue pot and heat until hot. Mix in the grated cheese and lemon juice.

2. Cook over a medium heat, stirring all the time, until the cheeses melt and the mixture just begins to bubble.

3. Blend the cornflour to a thin paste with the remaining 1 fl. oz (25 ml) of lager and add to the cheese mixture.

4. Cook slowly, still stirring, until the mixture comes to the boil and thickens to a smooth and creamy consistency. Do not over-boil or it may become stringy. Add the Vegemite and stir in thoroughly.

5. Stand the fondue pot over a spirit stove and eat straight away with cubes of bread.

Down-Under Fondue with an Oriental Touch
Make as above, but blend the cornflour with 1 tablespoon soy sauce and 1 tablespoon water instead of the extra fl. oz (25 ml) of lager. Use only 1 teaspoon Vegemite.

RUSSIAN FONDUE

Smoked cheese is much appreciated in Russia where they have their own version of Emmentel, lager is the top tipple and vodka the national spirit. How could this one fail.

SERVES 4

8 fl. oz (225 ml) lager
9 oz (250 g) smoked cheese (German or English), de-rinded and finely grated
7 oz (200 g) Emmental cheese, de-rinded and finely grated
2 level teaspoons cornflour
2 fl. oz (50 ml) vodka

FOR DIPPING
cubes of continental black bread

1. Pour the lager into the fondue pot and heat until hot. Mix in the grated cheeses.

2. Cook over a medium heat, stirring all the time, until the cheeses melt and the mixture just begins to bubble.

3. Blend the cornflour to a thin paste with the vodka and add to the cheese mixture.

4. Cook slowly, still stirring, until the mixture comes to the boil and thickens to a smooth and creamy consistency. Do not over-boil or it may become stringy.

5. Stand the fondue pot over a spirit stove and eat straight away with cubes of dark rye bread.

Russian Fondue with Caraway

Make as above, adding 1–2 teaspoons caraway seeds to the fondue pot at the same time as the cheese.

REVERSE FONDUE

*A*n off-beat idea which is edible fun for a clutch of 'elderly' teenagers and comprises tomato sauce into which cubes of cheese are dipped. Accompany with chips.

SERVES 6–8

1 jar (about 9 oz or 250 g) plain tomato sauce for pasta
1 fl. oz (25 ml) red wine

FOR DIPPING
8–12 oz (225–350 g) firm white cheese, such as Feta, Mozzarella,
Manchego, Provolone, etc.

TO ACCOMPANY

freshly fried chips

1. Tip the tomato sauce into the fondue pot. Add the wine and heat slowly, stirring, until the mixture comes to a gentle bubble. Leave over a low heat while you prepare the cheese.

2. Cut up the cheese into ½-inch (1-cm) cubes. Spear on to fondue forks, twirl round in the sauce and eat straight away.

SHORT-CUT FONDUES

*A*ll based on condensed soups with the addition of cheese and wine, these make supremely appetising fondues with the minimum of fuss. Serve with cubes of crusty brown bread.

SMOKED SALMON FONDUE

SERVES 4–5

1 can Gourmet Condensed Cream of Smoked Salmon Soup
6 fl. oz (175 ml) white wine
8 oz (225 g) Cheddar or Emmental cheese, de-rinded and finely grated

1. Heat the soup and wine in the fondue pot, stirring constantly until smooth.

2. Gradually add the grated cheese and continue to cook, stirring all the time, until the cheese melts.

3. Stand the fondue over a spirit stove and eat straight away with crusty brown bread.

Crab Bisque Fondue
Make as above, using a can of Gourmet Condensed Crab Bisque instead of the Cream of Smoked Salmon Soup.

Celery and Cider Fondue
Make as Smoked Salmon Fondue, using a can of Gourmet Condensed Cream of Celery Soup instead of the Smoked Salmon Soup and replacing the wine with an equal quantity of cider.

LE SAUCIER FONDUE

Le Saucier is a thermostatically controlled electric pan (see page 28). It is ideal for a hungry twosome who want a quick meal round an electric socket in the kitchen! You can make any of the savoury cheese fondues in Le Saucier; simply halve the quantity of ingredients and follow the method given below.

SERVES 2

4 fl. oz (125 ml) white wine
8 oz (225 g) Cheddar cheese, de-rinded and finely grated
1½ level teaspoons cornflour
1½ tablespoons spirit

FOR DIPPING
cubes of crusty French bread

1. Pour the wine into the Le Saucier pot and heat until hot, with the temperature set to Maximum (no. 5).

2. Gradually add the grated cheese.

3. Blend the cornflour to a thin paste with chosen spirit and add to the pot. Leave the paddle to rotate until the fondue is hot and just beginning to bubble.

4. Set the temperature to Low and remove the paddle. Put a stopper, such as a cork, into the funnel to stop any mixture falling in.

5. Eat from the pan with your chosen 'dippers', switching the pan off when the end is more or less in sight.

SAVOURY CHEESE FONDUES WITHOUT ALCOHOL

ENGLISH COUNTRY GARDEN FONDUE

A gentle fondue that is nice to eat outdoors on warm summer days. The wine is alcohol-free and there is a hint of subtlety coming from the ground bay leaves.

SERVES 4

9 fl. oz (250 ml) non-alcoholic wine
3½ oz (100 g) Lymeswold Brie, de-rinded and finely chopped
5 oz (150 g) Lymeswold Creamy White, de-rinded and finely chopped
8 oz Caerphilly cheese, de-rinded and finely chopped
1 level tablespoon cornflour
3 generous pinches of ground bay leaves

FOR DIPPING
cubes of Mixed Seed Bread (page 26)

1. Pour 8 fl. oz (225 ml) of the wine into the fondue pot and heat until hot. Mix in the cheeses.

2. Cook over a medium heat, stirring all the time, until the cheeses melt and the mixture just begins to bubble.

3. Blend the cornflour to a thin paste with the remaining 1 fl. oz (25 ml) of wine and add to the cheese mixture.

4. Cook slowly, still stirring, until the mixture comes to the boil and thickens to a smooth and creamy consistency. Do not over-boil or it may become stringy. Stir in the ground bay leaves.

5. Stand the fondue pot over a spirit stove and eat straight away with cubes of Caraway Seed Bread.

English Country Garden Fondue with Stilton
Make as above, substituting White Stilton for the Caerphilly cheese.

GOOD-HEALTH FONDUE

Stylish, simple and packed with essential vitamins and minerals, this apricot-coloured fondue is geared for those who are into healthy eating. Try with cubes of granary or wholemeal bread.

SERVES 4

8 fl. oz (225 ml) carrot juice
1 lb (450 g) Cheddar cheese, de-rinded and finely grated
1 level tablespoon cornflour
3 fl. oz (75 ml) milk
salt and pepper, to taste

FOR DIPPING
cubes of granary or wholemeal bread

1. Pour the carrot juice into the fondue pot and heat until hot. Add the grated cheese.

2. Cook over a medium heat, stirring all the time, until the cheese melts and the mixture just begins to bubble.

3. Blend the cornflour to a thin paste with the milk and add to the cheese mixture.

4. Cook slowly, still stirring, until the mixture comes to the boil and thickens to a smooth and creamy consistency. Do not over-boil or it may become stringy. Season to taste with salt and pepper.

5. Stand the fondue pot over a spirit stove and eat straight away with cubes of bread.

Good Health Fondue with Spice

Make as above, adding $\frac{1}{4}-\frac{1}{2}$ teaspoon ground nutmeg or mace at the same time as the salt and pepper.

A VERY PECULIAR MIXED BEAN FONDUE

This is an unusual and very wholesome fondue, full of fibre. It is best eaten lukewarm rather than hot with pieces of bread or toasted crumpet. To complete what is a fairly filling meal, serve with a salad and finish with fresh fruit.

SERVES 6–8

one 8-oz (225-g) can butter beans
one 11.6-oz (300-g) black-eyed beans
8 oz (225 g) Cheddar cheese, de-rinded and finely grated
2 level teaspoons salt
$\frac{1}{2}$ teaspoon garlic purée
4 fl. oz (125 ml) water
1 tablespoon lemon juice

FOR DIPPING
cubes of crusty white bread (page 24)
pieces of toasted crumpet

1. Blend both types of bean, with the liquor from their cans, to a smooth purée in a blender or food processor.

2. Place the bean purée into the fondue pot and heat until very hot, but not boiling, stirring constantly. Add the cheese, a handful at a time, and cook until melted.

3. Mix in the salt, garlic purée, water and lemon juice and reheat the fondue until hot, still stirring.

4. Leave until just lukewarm before eating with pieces of bread or toasted crumpet.

WELSH CAERPHILLY FONDUE

With a subtle tang and just off-white, this gives abstainers a chance to enjoy a made-to-measure fondue with either cubes of brown bread, freshly cooked baby new potatoes or florets of broccoli.

SERVES 4

8 fl. oz (225 ml) milk
1 lb (450 g) Caerphilly cheese, de-rinded and crumbled
1 garlic clove, peeled and crushed
1 teaspoon lemon juice
1 level tablespoon cornflour
1 fl. oz (25 ml) cold water
$\frac{1}{4}$ level teaspoon grated nutmeg

FOR DIPPING
cubes of homemade Orange and Date Bread (page 25)
hot new potatoes
florets of broccoli, par-boiled

1. Pour the milk into the fondue pot and heat until hot. Mix in the cheese, garlic and lemon juice.

2. Cook over a medium heat, stirring all the time, until the cheese melts and the mixture just begins to bubble.

3. Blend the cornflour to a thin paste with the water and add to the cheese mixture with the nutmeg.

4. Cook slowly, still stirring, until the mixture comes to the boil and thickens to a smooth and creamy consistency. Do not over-boil or it may become stringy.

5. Stand the fondue pot over a spirit stove and eat straight away with a selection of 'dippers'.

RICH SOFT CHEESE FONDUE WITH CHEDDAR

A classy fondue which is supremely smooth, flavourful and a whirl of golden cream. Try it with cubes of brown bread or baby new potatoes.

SERVES 4–5

14 oz (400 g) full-fat soft cheese
8 oz (225 g) jar medium Cheddar cheese spread
4 tablespoons milk
1 teaspoon prepared mustard

FOR DIPPING
cubes of homemade Onion Bread (page 26)
hot new potatoes

1. Put all the ingredients into the fondue pot.

2. Stir over a low heat until the mixture melts to a smooth, fairly thick and creamy consistency.

3. When the mixture is hot, but not boiling, transfer the fondue pot to a spirit stove and eat straight away with brown bread or new potatoes.

Rich Soft Cheese Fondue with English Mustard

Make as above, adding 2–3 teaspoons prepared English mustard, 2 teaspoons vinegar and 1 tablespoon finely chopped parsley just before serving.

HERBY CHEESE AND YOGURT FONDUE

This is quite a tangy and exquisitely creamy fondue, bursting with the aroma and flavour of fresh herbs.

SERVES 4–5

7 oz (200 g) full-fat soft cheese
8 oz (225 g) jar medium Cheddar cheese spread
8 oz (225 g) Greek sheep's milk yogurt with added cream
20 fresh tarragon leaves, finely chopped
7 fresh fennel fronds, finely chopped
5–6 fresh mint leaves, finely chopped
1 teaspoon finely chopped fresh oregano
8 chives, finely chopped

FOR DIPPING
pieces of Indian or Greek bread

1. Put all the ingredients into the fondue pot.

2. Stir over a low heat until the mixture melts to a smooth, fairly thick and creamy consistency.

3. When the mixture is hot, but not boiling, transfer the fondue pot to a spirit stove and eat straight away with pieces of bread.

ITALIAN RICOTTA FONDUE WITH RED PEPPERS

*S*weet red peppers and delicate white ricotta cheese create a pretty pale-orange fondue that is exquisitely mild. Eat with cubes of soft white bread.

one 6½-oz (185-g) can sweet red peppers
7 fl. oz (200 ml) milk
14 oz–1 lb (450–500 g) ricotta cheese
1 garlic clove
1½ level teaspoon salt
2 level teaspoons cornflour

FOR DIPPING
cubes of soft white bread or homemade Italian Bread (page 25)

1. Drain the red pepper liquid from the can directly into the fondue pot. Work the peppers to a fairly fine purée in a blender or food processor.

2. Add the puréed peppers and ¼ pint (150 ml) of the milk to the pot and slowly bring to the boil.

3. Keeping the heat fairly low, mix in the cheese, a little at a time, and stir briskly until it melts and forms a creamy mixture. Stir in the garlic and salt.

4. Blend the cornflour to a thin paste with the remaining 2 fl. oz (50 ml) milk, and add to the cheese mixture.

5. Bring just up to the boil, stirring all the time, then simmer gently for 1 minute.

6. Stand the fondue pot over a spirit stove and eat straight away with cubes of soft white bread.

SOUTHERN ITALIAN FONDUE

A rich contribution from Italy, characterful and warming, reasonably strong and seasoned with nutmeg, one of the most widely used spices in the country. Don't substitute alcohol for the milk as the cheeses will curdle. You have been warned!

SERVES 4

9 fl. oz (250 ml) milk
8 oz (225 g) Bel Paese cheese, de-rinded and finely chopped
8 oz (225 g) Pecorino cheese, de-rinded and finely grated
1 peeled and crushed garlic clove (optional)
1 level tablespoon cornflour
$\frac{1}{4}$ level teaspoon grated nutmeg

FOR DIPPING
cubes of homemade Lemon and Walnut Bread (page 25)

1. Pour 8 fl. oz (225 ml) of the milk into the fondue pot and heat until hot. Mix in the cheeses and garlic if using.

2. Cook over a medium heat, stirring all the time, until the cheeses melt and the mixture just begins to bubble.

3. Blend the cornflour to a thin paste with extra milk and add to the cheese mixture.

4. Cook slowly, still stirring, until the mixture comes to the boil and thickens to a smooth and creamy consistency. Do not over-boil or it may become stringy.

5. Stand the fondue pot over a spirit stove and eat straight away with cubes of brown bread.

Southern Italian Fondue with Tomatoes
Make as above, adding 3 medium-sized skinned and finely chopped tomatoes, seeds removed, after the fondue has thickened.

PIZZA FONDUE

A fondue designed for lovers of pizza, heaven with cubes of white bread and 'dippers' of cooked fennel, grilled bacon rolls and button mushrooms. It's a pretty colour too, a kind of apricot blush from the addition of tomato purée.

SERVES 4

$\frac{1}{2}$ *pint (275 ml) milk*
8 oz (225 g) Pecorino cheese, de-rinded and finely grated
8 oz (225 g) Mozzarella cheese, de-rinded and finely grated
1 level tablespoon cornflour
2 tablespoons tomato purée
$\frac{1}{4}$–$\frac{1}{2}$ *level teaspoon garlic purée*

FOR DIPPING
cubes of crusty white bread
pieces of cooked fennel
grilled bacon rolls
grilled button mushrooms

1. Pour 8 fl. oz (225 ml) of the milk into the fondue pot and heat until hot. Mix in the grated cheeses.

2. Cook over a medium heat, stirring all the time, until the cheeses melt and the mixture just begins to bubble.

3. Blend the cornflour to a thin paste with the remaining 2 fl. oz (50 ml) milk and add to the cheese mixture.

4. Cook slowly, still stirring, until the mixture comes to the boil and thickens to a smooth and creamy consistency. Work in the tomato and garlic purées. Do not over-boil or it may become stringy.

5. Stand the fondue pot over a spirit stove and eat straight away with a choice of 'dippers'.

Pizza Fondue with Olives

Make as above, adding 2 oz (50 g) stoned and finely chopped black olives to the thickened fondue.

Pizza Fondue with Onions

Make as Pizza Fondue, adding 2 oz (50 g) peeled and very finely chopped salad onions to the thickened fondue.

Pizza Fondue with Anchovies

Make as Pizza Fondue, adding 6 finely chopped canned anchovy fillets to the thickened fondue.

Pizza Fondue with Green Pepper

Make as Pizza Fondue, adding half a finely chopped small green pepper to the thickened fondue.

Pizza Fondue with Bacon

Make as Pizza Fondue, adding 2 oz (50 g) finely chopped and crisply fried bacon to the thickened fondue.

Pizza Fondue with Ham

Make as Pizza Fondue, adding 2 oz (50 g) finely chopped ham to the thickened fondue.

Pizza Fondue with Tuna

Make as Pizza Fondue, adding one small can (about $3\frac{1}{2}$ oz/100 g) finely mashed tuna to the thickened fondue. The brine or oil may be added as well.

SPANISH FONDUE

A gentle fondue, yet full-flavoured and creamy textured. Pleasant for those who appreciate mildness and made with one of Spain's favourite sheep's milk cheeses – Manchego.

SERVES 4

$\frac{1}{2}$ *pint (275 ml) milk*
8 oz (225 g) Manchego cheese, de-rinded and finely grated
8 oz (225 g) Emmental cheese, de-rinded and finely grated
1 level tablespoon cornflour

FOR DIPPING
cubes of homemade Lemon and Walnut Bread (page 25)

1. Pour 8 fl. oz (225 ml) of the milk into the fondue pot and heat until hot. Mix in the grated cheeses.

2. Cook over a medium heat, stirring all the time, until the cheeses melt and the mixture just begins to bubble.

3. Blend the cornflour to a thin paste with the remaining 2 fl. oz (50 ml) milk and add to the cheese mixture.

4. Cook slowly, still stirring, until the mixture comes to the boil and thickens to a smooth and creamy consistency. Do not over-boil or it may become stringy.

5. Stand the fondue pot over a spirit stove and eat straight away with cubes of bread.

Spanish Fondue with Saffron

Soak $\frac{1}{2}$ level teaspoon saffron strands in 2 fl. oz (25 ml) boiling water. Cool completely and strain. Make the fondue as above, using the saffron-flavoured water instead of milk to blend the cornflour to a thin paste.

Spanish Fondue with Olives

Make as Spanish Fondue, adding 3 oz (75 g) finely chopped stuffed olives after the fondue has thickened.

FRENCH FONDUE WITH GRAINY MUSTARD

This fresh tasting fondue combines 3 popular French cheeses with milk, garlic and mustard. A lively brew, it is one to bear in mind for teenage get-togethers.

SERVES 4

9 fl. oz (250 ml) milk
8 oz (225 g) Pyrénées cheese, de-rinded and finely grated
4 oz (125 g) Port Salut cheese, de-rinded and finely grated
4 oz (125 g) Tomme de Savoie cheese, de-rinded and finely grated
1 garlic clove, peeled and crushed
1 teaspoon lemon juice
2 teaspoons wholegrain mustard
1 level tablespoon cornflour

FOR DIPPING
cubes of assorted breads, such as homemade Mixed Seed Bread,
Anchovy and Chive Bread and Oriental Bread (pages 25–26)

1. Pour 8 fl. oz (225 ml) of the milk into the fondue pot and heat until hot. Mix in the grated cheeses, garlic, lemon juice and mustard.

2. Cook over a medium heat, stirring all the time, until the cheeses melt and the mixture just begins to bubble.

3. Blend the cornflour to a thin paste with the remaining 1 fl. oz (25 ml) milk and add to the cheese mixture.

4. Cook slowly, still stirring, until the mixture comes to the boil and thickens to a smooth and creamy consistency. Do not over-boil or it may become stringy.

5. Stand the fondue pot over a spirit stove and eat straight away with cubes of assorted breads.

Fondue Dijonnaise
Make as above, substituting 2 teaspoons Dijon mustard for the wholegrain mustard.

SMOKY GERMAN FONDUE

Elegant and ladylike, this German version of fondue is mild and delicate without a drop of alcohol in sight.

SERVES 4

11 fl. oz (300 ml) milk
10 oz (275 g) German smoked cheese, de-rinded and finely grated
6 oz (175 g) Emmental cheese, de-rinded and finely grated
1 level tablespoon cornflour

FOR DIPPING
cubes of dark-brown German or wholemeal bread
florets of cauliflower, par-boiled
cubes of celeriac, boiled

1. Pour 9 fl. oz (250 ml) of the milk into the fondue pot and heat until hot. Mix in the grated cheeses.

2. Cook over a medium heat, stirring all the time, until the cheeses melt and the mixture just begins to bubble.

3. Blend the cornflour to a thin paste with the remaining 2 fl. oz (50 ml) of milk, and add to the cheese mixture.

4. Cook slowly, still stirring, until the mixture comes to the boil and thickens to a smooth and creamy consistency. Do not over-boil or it may become stringy.

5. Stand the fondue pot over a spirit stove and eat straight away with a selection of 'dippers'.

Smoky German Fondue with Dill
Make as above and stir in 2 tablespoons finely chopped dill just before serving.

Smoky German Fondue with Paprika
Make as Smokey German Fondue and stir in $1\frac{1}{2}$ level teaspoons paprika just before serving.

GRECIAN GODDESS FONDUE

This is a wonderfully creamy fondue with a hint of mint. Serve with pieces of warm pitta bread or cubes of homemade Sesame and Fennel Seed Bread and acompany, Greek style, with individual salads of sliced tomatoes, sliced onions and black olives. To drink, try lemon tea but avoid alcohol which would drown out the delicacy of the fondue.

SERVES 6

one 8-oz (225-g) carton Greek sheep's yogurt with cream
$\frac{1}{4}$ pint (150 ml) milk
1 lb (450 g) Feta cheese, crumbled
1 level tablespoon cornflour
2 tablespoons water
1 teaspoon mint sauce

FOR DIPPING
pieces of warm pitta bread
cubes of homemade Sesame and Fennel Seed Bread (page 25)

1. Tip the yogurt and milk into the fondue pot and heat until hot. Mix in the crumbled cheese.

2. Cook over a medium heat, stirring all the time, until the cheese melts and the mixture just begins to bubble.

3. Blend the cornflour to a thin paste with the water and add to the cheese mixture.

4. Cook slowly, still stirring, until the mixture comes to the boil and thickens to a smooth and creamy consistency. Do not over-boil or it may become stringy. Stir in the mint sauce.

5. Stand the fondue pot over a spirit stove and eat straight away with pieces of pitta bread and Sesame Seed Bread.

Grecian Goddess Fondue with Lemon

Make as above, omitting the mint sauce but adding the finely grated peel of a small lemon.

MIDDLE EASTERN FONDUE

*I*nteresting because it's so different, and quite filling, this fondue will put you in a holiday mood.

SERVES 6–8

14 oz (400 g) hummus
9 oz (250 g) Greek strained yogurt
1 garlic glove, peeled and crushed
3 fl. oz (75 ml) milk
2 pinches of caster sugar
7 oz (200 g) Feta cheese, crumbled
3 oz (75 g) Halloumi cheese, de-rinded and finely grated

FOR DIPPING
pieces of pitta bread
cubes of homemade Sesame and Fennel Seed Bread (page 25)

1. Spoon the hummus into the fondue pot and add the yogurt, garlic, milk and sugar.

2. Cook over a medium heat, stirring constantly, until the mixture becomes smooth and hot. Do not allow to boil.

3. Mix in the cheese and continue to cook, still stirring, until the cheese melts and blends into the other ingredients completely.

4. Stand the fondue pot over a spirit stove and eat straight away with pitta and Sesame and Fennel Seed Bread.

Middle Eastern Fondue with Marjoram
Make as above, stirring in 2 tablespoons chopped fresh marjoram just before serving.

DUTCH FONDUE WITH MILK

Styled on kaarsdoop, Holland's traditional cheese melt, this fondue is alcohol-free, mild and takes well to the addition of fresh herbs (see variation below).

SERVES 4

$\frac{1}{2}$ pint (275 ml) milk
8 oz (225 g) Edam cheese, de-rinded and finely grated
8 oz (225 g) Gouda cheese, de-rinded and finely grated
$2\frac{1}{2}$ level teaspoons cornflour

FOR DIPPING

cubes of homemade Spicy Bread (page 25)

1. Pour 8 fl. oz (225 ml) of the milk into the fondue pot and heat until hot. Add the grated cheeses.

2. Cook over a medium heat, stirring all the time, until the cheeses melt and the mixture just begins to bubble.

3. Blend the cornflour to a smooth paste with the remaining 2 fl. oz (50 ml) milk, and add to the cheese mixture.

4. Cook slowly, still stirring, until the mixture comes to the boil and thickens to a smooth and creamy consistency. Do not over-boil or it may become stringy.

5. Stand the fondue pot over a spirit stove and eat straight away with cubes of brown bread.

Dutch Fondue with Milk and Herbs

Make as above, adding 3 tablespoons finely chopped fresh parsley, dill or coriander to the thickened fondue.

MILD NORWEGIAN FONDUE

This is a super 'high-tea' fondue and a joy eaten with pieces of fruit bread or currant buns. Also chunks of ripe banana and halved plums, especially Victorias.

SERVES 4

8 fl. oz (225 ml) milk
6 oz (175 g) Gjetost cheese, de-rinded and finely grated
7 oz (200 g) Ridder cheese, de-rinded and finely grated
4 oz (125 g) Jarlsberg cheese, de-rinded and finely grated
2 level teaspoons cornflour
1 fl. oz (25 ml) concentrated orange juice
2 pinches ground cinnamon

FOR DIPPING
pieces of fruit bread or currant buns
chunks of ripe banana
halved plums

1. Heat the milk in the fondue pot until hot. Add the grated cheese.

2. Cook over a medium heat, stirring all the time, until the cheeses melt and the mixture just begins to bubble.

3. Mix the cornflour to a thin paste with the orange juice then add to the cheese mixture.

4. Cook slowly, still stirring, until the mixture comes to the boil and thickens to a smooth and creamy consistency. Do not over-boil or it may become stringy.

5. Stand the fondue pot over a spirit stove and eat straight away with a choice of 'dippers'.

Mild Norwegian Fondue with Cranberries
Make as above, and stir 2 rounded tablespoons cranberry sauce into the thickened fondue.

SCANDINAVIAN BLACK CAVIAR FONDUE

A regal fondue speckled with black lumpfish caviar, not quite the real thing but tempting all the same at a fraction of the cost. Tinged pink with red grape juice and spiked with vodka, you can't go wrong with this one, especially if it is accompanied by cubes of dark brown continental bread, often available from Jewish delicatessens.

SERVES 4

8 fl. oz (225 ml) red grape juice
1 lb (450 g) Jarlsberg cheese, de-rinded and finely grated
1 garlic clove, peeled and crushed
one 2 oz (50 g) jar black Danish lumpfish caviar
1 level tablespoon cornflour
2 tablespoons vodka

FOR DIPPING
cubes of dark brown continental bread

1. Pour the grape juice into the fondue pot and heat until hot. Mix in the grated cheese, garlic and caviar.

2. Cook over a medium heat, stirring all the time, until the cheese melts and the mixture just begins to bubble.

3. Blend the cornflour to a thin paste with the vodka and add to the cheese mixture.

4. Cook slowly, still stirring, until the mixture comes to the boil and thickens to a smooth and creamy consistency. Do not over-boil or it may become stringy.

5. Stand the fondue pot over a spirit stove and eat straight away with cubes of bread.

Scandinavian Orange Caviar Fondue
Make as above, substituting orange lumpfish caviar for the black and using white grape juice instead of red.

Fondue Bourguignonne

*F*ondue Bourguignonne is a sumptuous fondue based on meat and poultry which some Swiss people describe as 'the most famous of them all.' Certainly it is rich and luxurious and makes a spectacular do-it-yourself meal cooked at the table. Pieces of meat or poultry are speared on to fondue forks and cooked in sizzling oil, then eaten with a variety of cold creamy sauces, favourite pickles and served, traditionally, with piping-hot chips and sometimes salad.

The Pot

The pot generally recommended for cooking the Fondue Bourguignonne should be deep and chimney shaped (wide at the base and narrower to the top) with a handle to the side. It must also be heavy and therefore sturdy enough to sit on top of the spirit stove without toppling, vital when one is dealing with very hot oil. The spirit stove, incidentally, is often the base of the fondue pot itself and sold with it as part of the package.

The Oil

Choose a quality oil such as sunflower or corn oil but avoid olive oil with its strong flavour and tendency to burn at high temperatures.

Half fill the fondue pot with the oil and heat on top of the cooker until sizzling. Carefully transfer the pot to a spirit stove at the table.

The Meat

Use top-quality beef – rump, fillet or sirloin – veal escalopes and chicken breasts. Cut the meat into thinnish squares with a sharp knife. The beef may be cut into slightly thicker slices (especially if it's preferred rare) or even small cubes. Make sure the meat is dry, otherwise the oil will splutter when the meat is added.

The Cooking

Taking it in turns (two at a time), spear a piece of meat or chicken on to a fondue fork. Carefully immerse in the hot oil and cook for 1–1½ minutes. Take out of the oil, transfer to a dinner plate and remove the meat with a fork. Dip into one of the sauces already on the plate and eat straight away.

THE BASIC RECIPE

SERVES 4

oil (see above)
1–1½ lb (450–750 g) meat or poultry (see above)
6 or 7 different sauces (see pages 94–9)
a selection of pickles and side dishes (see page 101)
freshly cooked chips

SAUCES

Based primarily on mayonnaise, these tend to be classic combinations with assorted additions. As an up-to-date alternative, yogurt may also be used as a cold sauce base (the nicest is Greek with added cream) or, for slimmers, low-fat natural yogurt. Also thick cream for non-dieters and puréed vegetables with added cream. The most convenient mayonnaise to use is obviously shop bought and there are some excellent brands round and about which are not dissimilar from homemade. However, for traditionalists who still want to make their own, some well-tried recipes follow.

TRADITIONAL MAYONNAISE

MAKES $\frac{1}{2}$ pint (275–300 ml)

2 egg yolks, size 1 or 2, at room temperature
$\frac{1}{2}$ level teaspoon salt
$\frac{1}{2}$ level teaspoon mustard powder
$\frac{1}{8}$ teaspoon caster sugar
white pepper, to taste
3 tablespoons lemon juice
$\frac{1}{2}$ pint (275 ml) salad oil, such as corn, groundnut, olive or sunflower oil
3 teaspoons boiling water

1. Place the egg yolks in a mixing bowl and stir in the salt, mustard powder, sugar and pepper.

2. Add 3 teaspoons of the lemon juice and beat thoroughly until smooth and evenly mixed.

3. Start beating in the oil, drop by drop, until the mayonnaise is as thick as whipped cream. By this time half to two-thirds of the oil should have been beaten in.

4. Add 2 more teaspoons lemon juice then, still beating, add the rest of the oil in a slow continuous stream.

5. Mix in the remaining lemon juice and the water. Scrape into a jar or dish, then cover and refrigerate until required.

Mayonnaise with More Bite

Make as above, but replace half the lemon juice with wine or cider vinegar. Alternatively use all vinegar.

Luxury Mayonnaise

Make as for Mayonnaise, but replace 2 teaspoons oil with 2 teaspoons walnut or hazelnut oil.

Mayonnaise with a Continental Taste

Make as for Mayonnaise, but replace the mustard powder with 1 teaspoon Dijon mustard.

BLENDER MAYONNAISE WITHOUT EGG

*I*t is almost impossible to go wrong with this recipe if you have a blender and the result is a delicious, thick mayonnaise-cum-salad cream which is gloriously smooth and takes about 2 minutes to make. Note that it thickens up more on standing.

MAKES 6 fl. oz(175 ml)

7 tablespoons salad oil, such as corn, groundnut, olive or sunflower
1 oz (25 g) instant non-fat milk granules, such as Marvel
4 tablespoons hot water
$\frac{1}{2}$ level teaspoon salt
$\frac{1}{2}$ level teaspoon mustard powder
white pepper, to taste
2 tablespoons red wine vinegar
$\frac{1}{8}$ teaspoon caster sugar

1. Place all the ingredients in a blender goblet and fit the lid on securely.

2. Blend at high speed for 30 seconds. Remove the lid and scrape the mixture down the sides of the goblet.

3. Replace the lid and blend at high speed for a further 30 seconds. The mayonnaise should now be quite thick.

4. Spoon into a dish, cover and refrigerate until required.

RIGHT: Smoked Salmon Fondue (see page 73)

BLENDER MAYONNAISE WITH EGG

Another effortless recipe that includes a whole egg and turns out thick and gleaming with a slightly lighter texture than Traditional Mayonnaise. This factor is probably due to the egg white.

MAKES $\frac{1}{2}$ pint (275–300 ml)

one egg, size 1
$\frac{1}{2}$ level teaspoon mustard powder or 1 level teaspoon Dijon mustard
$\frac{1}{2}$ level teaspoon salt
pinch of cayenne pepper or 2 drops of Tabasco sauce
$\frac{1}{4}$ level teaspoon caster sugar
$\frac{1}{2}$ pint (275 ml) salad oil, such as corn, groundnut, olive or sunflower
2 tablespoons wine or cider vinegar
2 teaspoons lemon juice
3 teaspoons boiling water

1. Break the egg into a blender goblet, then add the mustard, salt, pepper or Tabasco sauce, sugar and 4 tablespoons of the oil. Place the lid on securely.

2. Cover and blend at high speed for $\frac{1}{2}$ minute.

3. Reduce the speed to medium, remove the lid and gradually add two-thirds of the remaining oil and all the vinegar.

4. Blend until thick and smooth. Slowly add the remaining oil and the lemon juice. Continue to blend for about $\frac{1}{2}$ minute.

5. Scrape into a dish, then stir in the water. Cover and chill until required.

OVERLEAF: *Fondue Bourguignonne (see page 93)*

TO FLAVOUR THE MAYONNAISE

*W*hen serving a selection of the sauces below, divide the ordinary mayonnaises into quarters and the mayonnaise without egg in half. Add the following to each quarter or half and offer 3 to 4 sauces from which to choose. These should be spooned on to dinner plates and eaten with the fried meat or poultry, etc.

Cocktail Sauce
Mix in 2 teaspoons tomato purée, $\frac{1}{2}$ teaspoon horseradish sauce, $\frac{1}{4}$ teaspoon Worcestershire sauce and 2 drops Tabasco sauce or a pinch of cayenne pepper.

Dill Sauce
Mix in 2 slightly rounded teaspoons finely chopped fresh dill.

Leek Sauce
Mix in 1 tablespoon finely chopped leek that has been first blanched in boiling water for 1 minute, then drained thoroughly.

Garlic and Chive Sauce
Mix in $\frac{1}{4}$ teaspoon garlic purée and 1 tablespoon finely chopped fresh chives.

Curry Sauce
Mix in $\frac{1}{2}$–1 level teaspoon mild curry powder.

Ravigote Sauce
Mix in $\frac{1}{2}$ teaspoon each of fresh chopped tarragon, chives, parsley and chervil or marjoram if available.

Mustard Sauce
Mix in $\frac{1}{4}$ level teaspoon French mustard.

Sauce Andalouse
Mix in 2 teaspoons tomato purée and 2 teaspoons finely chopped canned red pimiento.

Epicure Sauce
Mix in $1\frac{1}{2}$ teaspoons finely chopped gherkins and 2 teaspoons chutney.

Sauce Verte
Mix in 2 teaspoons finely chopped fresh parsley and the same of chopped fresh tarragon, chives and spinach leaves.

Rémoulade
Mix in $\frac{1}{2}$ teaspoon anchovy sauce or anchovy purée, $\frac{1}{4}$ teaspoon mustard (French for preference), $\frac{1}{2}$ teaspoon each of finely chopped fresh parsley, tarragon and chervil, $\frac{1}{2}$ teaspoon chopped gherkins and $\frac{1}{2}$ teaspoon chopped capers.

Russian Sauce
Mix in $\frac{1}{4}$ teaspoon finely grated horseradish (this can be bought ready-prepared) or $\frac{1}{2}$ teaspoon horseradish sauce, 2 teaspoons tomato ketchup, 1 teaspoon peeled and finely grated onion, 2 teaspoons double cream.

Thousand Island Sauce
Mix in 1 shelled and finely chopped hard-boiled egg (size 4), $\frac{1}{4}-\frac{1}{2}$ teaspoon chilli sauce or 1 teaspoon tomato ketchup, 2 teaspoons finely chopped stuffed olives, 1 teaspoon each finely chopped fresh parsley and chives, 1 tablespoon whipped cream or thick double cream.

Pickles and Side Dishes

Offer a selection of 6 or more pickles and side dishes to accompany the meat and sauces. The first five given below are a typical Swiss selection. Arrange them attractively in individual dishes.

Cocktail gherkins

Baby corn on the cob, left whole

Fresh seasonal firm fruits, prettily cut and artistically arranged on a platter

Canned artichoke hearts, drained

Mustard fruits. These are idiosyncratic and are sweet glacé fruits impregnated with mustard. They are widely eaten in Italy and apparently Switzerland and available only from a limited number of specialist food shops. I suggest you serve one or two glacé fruits with a small pot of English mustard to accompany. Eaten together you'll have a smattering of the real thing.

Pickled silverskin onions

Slices of pickled cucumber

Pickled walnuts

Mixed vegetables pickled in vinegar

Pickled red cabbage

Stuffed olives

Cherry tomatoes

Radicchio leaves

Radishes

Sweetcorn relish

Plum chutney

Tomato chutney

Ketchup

Fondue Chinoise

*T*his is a Swiss speciality fondue with Chinese overtones and related to the Mongolian Hot Pot (also known as Shabu-Shabu, Chinese Hot Pot and Chinese Fire Pot).

The technique of preparation, followed by dipping and eating, is much like the Fondue Bourguignonne but this time the cooking medium is stock not oil. The chosen food is simmered in the very hot liquid until ready to suit personal taste, then dipped into a selection of sauces and served with rice. Glass or Chinese noodles, almost white in colour and thin, can be used instead of rice but they need soaking before cooking – follow pack directions most carefully or you'll end up with a sticky mess if you don't. The forks can be long fondue ones or chopsticks.

The Pot

The ideal pot to use for a Fondue Chinoise is chimney shaped (narrow at the base and widening towards the top) with a handle to one side. It must be heavy and sturdy enough to sit securely on top of a spirit stove without tipping over and splashing hot liquid over the table and diners. The capacity of the pot should be about $2\frac{1}{2}$ pints (1.5 litres). If your pot is smaller, use less stock.

The Stock

For the best flavour, use one of the homemade stock recipes given on pages 104–5. If you are short of time, however, there are several other kinds of stock, quickly made, which will suffice:

Stock cubes and water

Bouillon cubes and water

Condensed consommé in cans, diluted as instructed

Stock powder (sometimes all vegetable) combined with water as directed.

The Meat

Use top-quality rump cuts of beef and pork. Also chicken and turkey breast meat. Cut into thin squares with a sharp knife. The beef should be cut into thicker slices or cubes if it is preferred underdone. Small pieces of chicken or duck liver would make a rich contribution to Fondue Chinoise. Tasty and economical are homemade meatballs (see page 106).

The Cooking

Spear the meat, liver and/or meatball, a piece at a time, on to a fondue fork or hold safely between chopsticks. Immerse into the gently bubbling stock and cook for about $1\frac{1}{2}$ minutes. Take out of the stock, transfer to a dinner plate and eat straight away. Either take the meat off the fondue fork and eat with a dinner fork or keep to chopsticks.

THE BASIC RECIPE

SERVES 4

$2\frac{1}{2}$ (1.5 litres) pints beef, chicken or vegetable stock (see opposite and
pages 104–5)
$1-1\frac{1}{2}$ lb (450–700 g) meat or poultry, or one quantity of meatballs
(see opposite and page 106)
8 oz (225 g) rice or 8 oz (225 g) Chinese noodles, cooked (quantities
given are for uncooked rice or noodles)
a minimum of 8 or 9 sauces (see pages 98–9 and 107)
a selection of pickles and side dishes (see page 107)

STOCKS

BEEF STOCK
——— ✍ ———

MAKES ABOUT 2½ pints (1.5 litres)

8 oz (225 g) lean beef bones
2½ pints (1.5 litres) water
6 oz (150 g) carrots, peeled and thickly sliced
3 oz (75 g) turnip, peeled and cut into large cubes
4 oz (125 g) swede, peeled and cut into large cubes
2 medium leeks, washed, trimmed and halved lengthways
2 celery sticks, cut in short pieces
3 level teaspoons salt
1 bouquet garni
1 bay leaf

1. Put the bones and water into a large pan and bring slowly to the boil. Skim off any scum when it rises to the surface.

2. Add the vegetables to the stock and bring to the boil. Skim thoroughly if necessary, then lower the heat and cover tightly.

3. Simmer for 2½ hours, taking care not to let the pan boil dry; top up with a little boiling water now and then if necessary.

4. Remove from the heat and strain into a clean bowl. When completely cold, cover and refrigerate overnight.

5. Before using, remove any fat that has set on the top. Transfer the stock to a saucepan and bring to the boil. Carefully pour into the fondue pot.

Beef Stock made in the Pressure Cooker
Place all the ingredients in a pressure cooker. Bring to the boil and skim the surface. Cover and pressure cook at full pressure for 45 minutes. Complete steps 4 and 5 of the previous recipe.

Extra Beef Stock

For extra flavour, add 8 oz (225 g) beef shin meat, left in one piece, to the stock pot with the bones. Afterwards the meat can be minced and used for shepherds' pie.

CHICKEN STOCK

*F*ollow the recipe for Beef Stock opposite, using half a chicken instead of the beef bones and cooking for 1 hour instead of $2\frac{1}{2}$ hours (or for 20 minutes in a pressure cooker). The chicken meat can be cut-up and used in pies or salad.

VEGETABLE STOCK

*F*ollow the recipe for Beef Stock opposite, but omit the beef bones. Cook for 45 minutes only (or 20 minutes in a pressure cooker). Strain into a clean bowl. Keep the vegetables to make a purée to use as the base for a cream soup.

MEATBALLS

These are a bit fiddly to put together but are worth the effort.

For speed, you can part-fry the meatballs first in a little oil, allowing about 5 minutes and turning over twice. They will need a further 15–20 seconds in the stock. If cooked in the stock from raw, allow $1\frac{1}{2}$ minutes for each.

A THOUGHT

Avoid ready-prepared minced beef. It's still on the fatty side and could make the stock greasy. Chuck is a good-quality, lean cut and ideal for these particular meatballs. Shin of beef is also excellent but is a tough cut and should be passed through the mincer twice to break down the fibres.

MAKES APPROXIMATELY 80

1 lb (450 g) chuck steak, either minced for you by the butcher or at home
2 oz (50 g) fresh white or brown breadcrumbs
2 oz (50 g) onion, peeled and finely grated
one egg, size 3, beaten
1 level teaspoon salt
freshly milled black or white pepper to taste

1. Place the minced beef in a bowl and using a fork, mix in the breadcrumbs, onion, egg, salt and pepper.

2. When thoroughly mixed, roll into about 80 marble-sized balls.

SAUCES

Offer your guests at least 8 or 9 sauces. I suggest serving 5 or 6 of the mayonnaise-based sauces on pages 94–9, in addition to a selection of the following ready-prepared sauces:

Soy sauce

Chilli sauce

Oyster sauce

Brown ketchup hotted up with a few drops of Tabasco

Bought or homemade sweet-sour sauce

Chutney

PICKLES AND SIDE DISHES

Offer a selection of pickles and side dishes to accompany the meat. They are very much a matter of personal taste, but the first five given below are a typical Swiss selection.

Black mushrooms or canned Chinese straw mushrooms (which are quite small and beautifully delicate)

Canned bamboo shoots, cut into pieces

Canned palm hearts, cut into pieces

Mustard fruits (see page 100)

Canned water chestnuts, halved

Bean sprouts

Spring onions, finely chopped or shredded

Preserved ginger, drained and finely chopped

Mixed vegetables pickled in vinegar

Mange tout (the Chinese snowpeas), par-boiled

FISH FONDUE CHINOISE

Lighter than meat and of special appeal to all those who are fish converts.

The Stock
Follow the recipe for Beef Stock (page 104), but use $1\frac{1}{2}$ lb (750 g) fish trimmings instead of the beef bones, and omit the turnip and swede. Cook for one hour.

The Fish
I suggest you serve the following selection of fish. Allow approximately 6 oz (175 g) per person. The assortment is up to individual taste. Poach the fish in the stock.

Shelled prawns

Pieces of scallops

Small cubes of fresh salmon, skinned

Small cubes of monk fish, skinned

Small pieces of hake, skinned

Small pieces of Dover sole, skinned

The fish should be speared on fondue forks and lightly cooked in the stock. Allow about 1 minute per piece as over-cooking will toughen the fish. Dip into sauces. I suggest the following selection:

Tartare sauce

Thousand Island

Greek yogurt with finely
    chopped walnuts and
    salt to taste

Soy sauce

Ketchup

Worcestershire sauce.

Sweet Fondues

*T*he ultimate decadent dessert; rich, rich, rich, sweet as honey and devastatingly calorie laden but balanced out to some extent by the fresh fruits used for dipping. Quick and easy to make and visually impressive, it's another Swiss masterpiece of gastronomic ingenuity and a stunning way to end a dinner party meal. Chocolate rules but other things also melt down well, like fudge and marshmallows, adding a new dimension to the strictly chocolate fondue so beloved by the Swiss.

FRUIT FOR DIPPING

But first the fruits. In order for the fondue mixture to coat evenly, peel should always be removed and soft fruits, like raspberries, avoided as they will become a squash in no time. The syrup round canned fruits will also stop the fondue from adhering, so rinse and dry before dipping. Fruits to use — a few suggestions:

Fresh lychees, stones removed

Whole strawberries

Cubes of fresh mango, peeled

Cubes of paw-paw (papaya), peeled

Melon balls

Cubes of watermelon

Halved plums, peeled and stones removed

Halved greengages, peeled and stones removed

Pieces of fresh nectarine, peeled

Cubes of apple, peeled and sprinkled with lemon juice

Cubes of slightly underripe pears, peeled and sprinkled with lemon juice

Chunks of banana, sprinkled with lemon juice

Cubes of fresh pineapple

Segments of orange

Segments of grapefruit

White Toblerone Fondue

*F*ondue and Swiss Toblerone make a perfect match – how about this.

SERVES 4–6

14 oz (400 g) bar of White Toblerone chocolate, kitchen temperature
4 tablespoons single cream
1 tablespoon Grand Marnier or orange liqueur

1. Break up the chocolate and put into a small copper pan or miniature fondue pot. Add the cream.

2. Place over a low heat and stir constantly until the chocolate has melted.

3. Mix in the liqueur thoroughly, then stand the pan or fondue pot on top of a low-powered heater to keep warm; a night light in a holder is adequate.

4. Spear fruit or fruits on to fondue forks, dip into the chocolate and eat straight away.

Other Fruit liqueurs to try
Apricot, banana, cherry brandy, peach, Midori (melon), and mandarin

Dark Toblerone Fondue
Make as above, using dark Toblerone chocolate instead of white and brandy instead of the Grand Marnier.

Milk Chocolate Toblerone Fondue
Make as above, using milk chocolate Toblerone instead of white chocolate Toblerone and coffee or any nut liqueur instead of the Grand Marnier.

CHOCOLATE CHOCOLATE FONDUE

*D*ark, daring and sensual. As smooth as velvet. Outstandingly understated.

SERVES 4–6

14 oz (400 g) plain chocolate
5 tablespoons single cream

FOR DIPPING
a selection of fruit (page 110)

1. Break the chocolate into a small copper pan or miniature fondue pot and add the cream.

2. Place over a low heat and stir constantly until the chocolate has melted.

3. Stand the pan or fondue pot on top of a low-powered heater to keep warm; a night light in a holder is adequate. Eat straight away.

Chocolate Chocolate Fondue with Hazelnuts
Make as above, adding 1 oz (25 g) toasted and finely chopped hazelnuts just before serving.

Chocolate Chocolate Fondue with Whisky
Make as Chocolate Chocolate Fondue, but reduce the quantity of cream to 4 tablespoons and add 1 tablespoon of whisky when the chocolate has melted.

Chocolate Chocolate Fondue with Mint
Make as Chocolate Chocolate Fondue, but reduce the quantity of cream to 4 tablespoons and add 1 tablespoon of mint liqueur when the chocolate has melted.

Chocolate Chocolate Fondue with Rum
Make as Chocolate Chocolate Fondue, but reduce the quantity of cream to 4 tablespoons and add 1 tablespoon dark rum when the chocolate has melted.

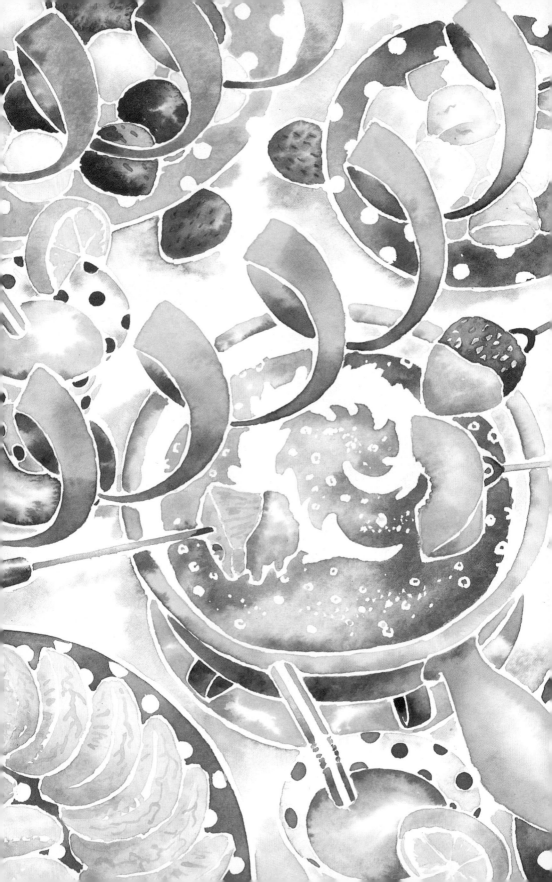

STRAWBERRIES AND CREAM FONDUE

*M*idsummer madness is a whirl of sophistication – my favourite of all.

SERVES 4–6

14 oz (400 g) chocolate bar with strawberry cream filling
4 tablespoons single cream
1 tablespoon strawberry liqueur or syrup

FOR DIPPING
a selection of fruit (page 110)

1. Break the chocolate into a small copper pan or miniature fondue pot and add the cream.

2. Place over a low heat and stir constantly until the chocolate has melted.

3. Mix in the liqueur or syrup thoroughly, then stand the pan or fondue pot on top of a low-powered heater to keep warm; a night light in a holder is adequate. Eat straight away.

PREVIOUS PAGE: Fondue Chinoise (see pages 101–8)
LEFT: Fudge Fondue (see page 114)

FUDGE FONDUE

*A*ll sweetness and light and a blissful contrast with sharpish fruit like oranges and grapefruit.

SERVES 4–6

12 oz (350 g) vanilla fudge
4 tablespoons single cream

FOR DIPPING
a selection of fresh fruit (page 110)

1. Break the fudge into a small copper pan or miniature fondue pot and add the cream.

2. Place over a low heat and stir constantly until the fudge has melted.

3. Stand the pan or fondue pot on top of a low-powered heater to keep warm; a night light in a holder is adequate. Eat straight away.

Boozy Fudge Fondue

Make as above but reduce the amount of cream by 1 tablespoon and add 1 tablespoon of any of the following tipples: sherry or Madeira, brandy, orange liqueur, Drambuie or any other herb liqueur, banana liqueur.

Nutty Fudge Fondue

Make as Fudge Fondue or Boozy Fudge Fondue and stir in 1 oz (25 g) very finely chopped pecan nuts when the fudge has melted.

Fruit and Nut Fudge Fondue

Make as Fudge Fondue or Boozy Fudge Fondue and stir in $\frac{1}{2}$ oz (15 g) very finely chopped walnuts and $\frac{1}{2}$ oz (15 g) raisins when the fudge has melted.

Fudge Fondue with Ginger

Make as Fudge Fondue or Boozy Fudge Fondue and stir in 1 oz (25 g) finely chopped preserved ginger.

MARSHMALLOW FONDUE

*L*ight and bright, pleasant after a rich meal. Eat with pieces of banana. Use your favourite fruit liqueur – orange, apricot, banana, strawberry or peach.

SERVES 4–6

14 oz (400 g) pink and white marshmallows
1 tablespoon single cream
1 tablespoon liqueur to taste

FOR DIPPING
chunks of banana

1. Put the marshmallows into a small copper pan or miniature fondue pot with the cream and liqueur.

2. Place over a low heat and stir constantly until the marshmallows have melted.

3. Stand the pan or pot on top of a low-powered heat to keep warm; a night light in a holder is adequate. Eat straight away.

WHITE CHOCOLATE FONDUE
WITH WALNUTS

Gloriously creamy, a classy fondue laced with walnuts and peach or apricot brandy.

SERVES 4–6

14 oz (400 g) white chocolate
4 tablespoons single cream
1 tablespoon peach or apricot brandy
$\frac{1}{2}$ oz (15 g) walnuts, very finely chopped

FOR DIPPING
a selection of fresh fruit (page 110)

1. Break the chocolate into a small copper pan or miniature fondue pot and add the cream.

2. Place over a low heat and stir constantly until the chocolate has melted.

3. Mix in the liqueur thoroughly, then stand the pan or fondue pot on top of a low-powered heater to keep warm; a night light in a holder is adequate. Eat straight away.

White Chocolate and Coffee Fondue
Make as above but add 1 tablespoon coffee liqueur instead of the brandy.

Sweet Cheese Fondue

*R*ather like an uncooked cheesecake mixture, this one is a joy with cubes of fruit bread, chunks of banana and pieces of canned pineapple.

SERVES 6

7 fl. oz (200 ml) milk
1 lb (450 g) medium-fat soft curd cheese, at room temperature
2 oz (50 g) caster sugar
1 level tablespoon cornflour
2 pinches of salt
$\frac{1}{2}$ teaspoon vanilla essence
2 egg yolks from size 1 or 2 eggs, at room temperature

FOR DIPPING
cubes of fruit bread or malt bread
boudoir biscuits (crisp sponge fingers)
pieces of banana
pieces of pineapple

1. Plus 5 fl. oz (150 ml) of the milk into the fondue pot and bring slowly to the boil.

2. Keeping the heat low, add the cheese a little at a time, stirring briskly between each addition until it melts down to form a creamy mixture with the milk. Stir in the sugar.

3. Blend the cornflour to a smooth paste with the remaining 2 fl. oz (50 ml) milk. Whisk in the salt, vanilla essence and yolks.

4. Add to the cheese mixture and bring just up to the boil, stirring all the time. Simmer gently for 1 minute.

5. Stand the fondue pot over a spirit stove and eat straight away.

Sweet Cheese Fondue with Citrus
Make as above, adding 1 teaspoon finely grated lime, lemon or orange rind just before serving.

HONEY BUNNY FONDUE

I wrote a note to myself when I tasted the fondue for the first time – 'marvellous, like cream', it said and so it is. It's tinted a delicate pink and blissful with cubed scones.

SERVES 4–6

7 oz (200 g) full-fat soft cheese
8 oz (225 g) Greek yogurt with added cream
3 tablespoons honey
2 tablespoons redcurrant jelly, room temperature

FOR DIPPING
cubes of fruit or plain scones

1. Put the cheese and yogurt into the fondue pot and place over a low heat until hot but not boiling.

2. Add the honey and redcurrant jelly and stir until melted.

3. Stand the fondue pot over a spirit stove and eat straight away.

Fruit Bunny Fondue
Make as above, using 3 tablespoons of seedless jam instead of the honey.

Apple Purée Fondue

Fruit purées make unusual and healthy fondues, packed with vitamins. You can vary the flavouring in this Apple Purée Fondue by using a teaspoon of grated lemon or orange rind or $\frac{1}{2}$ teaspoon vanilla essence instead of the cinnamon and mixed spice.

Serves 4–6

1 lb (450 g) cooking apples, peeled, cored and sliced
3 tablespoons water
$\frac{1}{2}$ level teaspoon ground cinnamon or mixed spice
2–4 oz (50–125 g) sugar to taste

For Dipping
marshmallows
chunks of banana
firm pear slices

1. Place the apple, water and cinnamon or mixed spice in a large saucepan and bring to the boil. Cover the pan and simmer over a low heat for 4–6 minutes until the apple is soft.

2. Beat the fruit to a purée with a wooden spoon, then beat in the sugar to taste.

3. Transfer the apple purée into the fondue pot and place over a medium heat until the purée is hot. Place the fondue pot on a spirit stove and eat straight away.

Rhubarb Fondue

Make as above but replace the apples with $1\frac{1}{2}$ lb (700 g) rhubarb and omit the cinnamon or mixed spice. Cook carefully and, when soft, blend to a smooth purée in a food processor or blender.

Acknowledgements

Sonia Allison would like to thank the following for their cooperation:

The Swiss Centre, Campbell's Soups, Brown & Polson, Danish Cheeses, Dutch Cheeses, Colman's Mustard, Holsten Pils Lager, Lee & Perrins, Mazola Oil, Le Creuset Fondue Pots and Le Saucier.

Index